PORTFOLIO

PANDEYMONIUM

Piyush Pandey, sixty, is the executive chairman and creative director for Ogilvy & Mather India and South Asia, and the winner of over 600 awards for advertising. Born and raised in Jaipur, Piyush did his schooling from St. Xavier's School, and obtained his master's from St. Stephen's College, Delhi. He is passionate about cricket, having played in the Ranji Trophy, representing Rajasthan. His first job was as a tea taster, before he joined Ogilvy in 1982 as trainee account executive.

Piyush has been named The Most Influential Man in Indian Advertising ten years in a row by the *Economic Times*. In 2000, the Ad Club of Mumbai voted his commercial for the adhesive brand Fevikwik The Commercial of the Century, and his work on Cadbury as The Campaign of the Century. He was voted Asia's Creative Person of the Year at the Media Asia Awards 2002. He is the only Indian to have won a double gold at Cannes and a triple Grand Prize at the London International Awards. Ogilvy India has won over fifty lions at Cannes under his leadership. In 2002, he won India's first-ever Silver Pencil at The One Show Awards and was named the president of the jury for Outdoor & Press and Film at the Cannes Lion International Advertising Festival, 2004, which was a first for an Asian. In 2007, Piyush was inducted into the Hall of Fame by the Communication Arts Guild. In 2009, the New York Advertising Festival presented Piyush the prestigious Creative Achievement Award. He was awarded the Lifetime Achievement Award in 2010 by the Advertising Agencies Association of India. He became the only Indian to get the Lifetime Achievement at the CLIO Awards, New York, in 2012.

PRAISE FOR THE BOOK

'Piyush is full of creative energy, ideas and humour, and this is what is reflected in *Pandeymonium*. A must-read for people in the consumption and advertising space to learn what desi communication means and how effective it is'—Kishore Biyani, CEO, Future Group

'An easy and compelling read. Great insights from a genius who is grounded and with a rare sense of the real'—Arun Lal, former cricketer and commentator

'A fantastic lesson on how the simple experiences of a life's journey make for an outstanding advertising legend. A must-read for all advertising professionals'—Rajeev Bakshi, MD and vice president, METRO Cash and Carry India

PANDEYMONIUM

PIYUSH PANDEY ON ADVERTISING

PORTFOLIO
PENGUIN
An imprint of Penguin Random House

PORTFOLIO

USA | Canada | UK | Ireland | Australia
New Zealand | India | South Africa | China

Portfolio is part of the Penguin Random House group of companies
whose addresses can be found at global.penguinrandomhouse.com

Published by Penguin Random House India Pvt. Ltd.
4th Floor, Capital Tower 1, MG Road,
Gurugram 122 002, Haryana, India

Penguin
Random House
India

First published in Portfolio by Penguin Books India 2015

All images and television commercials mentioned in this book are available
for viewing on www.pandeymonium.in

10 9

The views and opinions expressed in this book are the author's own and the facts
are as reported by him which have been verified to the extent possible, and the
publishers are not in any way liable for the same.

ISBN 9780143427650

For sale in India only

Typeset in Sabon by Manipal Digital Systems, Manipal
Printed at Replika Press Pvt. Ltd, India

www.penguin.co.in

FSC
www.fsc.org
MIX
Paper from
responsible sources
FSC® C016779

To my late parents, Indra Narayan Pandey and Bhagwati Pandey, for giving me the opportunity to actualize myself. I'm also grateful to them for giving me a family of seven sisters and a brother who added values and nuances to everything I'm proud of today.
I wish my parents were around to read this book.
I pray that it is available in God's Library.

*

On the professional front, I would like to dedicate this book to my late boss, Suresh Mullick, who discovered and adopted me in the creative department of Ogilvy. Suresh trusted me enough to get me to write the lyrics of his masterpiece, '*Mile sur mera tumhara*'.

Contents

A Note from the Author

After considering many options for crediting my friend Anant Rangaswami for this book, I decided on the title Curator. The dictionary meaning of a curator is an 'overseer, manager, guardian, and content specialist, responsible for an institution's collections and involved with the interpretation of heritage material'. However, I found the legal explanation more appropriate. It defines a curator as 'a guardian of a minor, lunatic, or other incompetent, especially with regard to his or her property'. This is what Anant has been for me.

First Anant pestered me for two years to write a book. And then one day, he convinced me over a drink. We disappeared for a week to my home in Goa. We worked from 6 a.m. to 6 p.m. every day. Anant interrogated me, cajoled me, coaxed me, and recorded me. He walked down my memory lane with me. He asked me a million questions, and helped me jog my memory. We cried together in moments of nostalgia and rolled on the floor with laughter in moments of joy. This was the week when the skeleton of the book was created.

Over the next six months, we worked weekends, squeezed a couple of hours at odd times. I wrote, he edited, sometimes even changed it.

Many thanks, Anant, for your guidance and partnership.

Piyush Pandey
August 2015, Bombay

Foreword

There are perhaps no days of our childhood we lived so fully as those we spent with a favourite book.

Hundreds of books on the subject of advertising are released almost every day. But there are some that stand the test of time and remain 'required reading'.

Pandeymonium, Piyush Pandey's book on the subject, is one such book.

If you have a passion for the art and the ability of communication or anything related, start digging into this book for great ideas. Piyushji has written his book in a laid-back, informative manner, filled with examples of powerful and effective creative briefs. My knowledge and experience in this line being questionable, I found myself drawn to the subject almost trance-like—that is how easy and enjoyable the read was. Entertaining, with stories about his experiences in the industry—no heavy academic theory—it is about how society is becoming smarter and how our brain is evolving to prepare us for the future.

Those just getting into the business will find a step-by-step guide in here to every aspect of advertising. For those already in this line, the book will not only make you laugh and cry, but help you pick up tips and reminders that may make you an even better creative professional. It is a vivid memoir of Piyush Pandey, which, you will concur in time, is a gem meant to be placed on the Ogilvy bookshelf.

The rules for parents are but three: love, limit, and let them be. Piyushji, as a parent of the advertising world, teaches us in this book to love what you are doing, to know your limitations, and when to let things be.

Advertising is his 'home', a home where respect for space and honest engagement are at the core; they make for a strong anchor for the family to be a happy commune, explaining how things work, have cause and effect, all in the day-to-day tasks of working in this field.

There is a clear respect and appreciation for the written word in this book; holding it, you feel like turning its pages with anticipation, finding a favourite bookmark to treasure, and reading it aloud during quiet moments.

One might like to think that with focus, determination and hard work, one can orchestrate the perfect outcome for all situations, but life, with its menu of complexities, will most certainly deal a hand you were not anticipating. It is how one deals with this type of situation that makes all the difference.

The books that help you the most are those which make you think the most. The hardest way of learning is by way of easy reading, and *Pandeymonium* is that ship of thought, deep freighted with truth and passion for its subject matter.

This book does not require an audience with a certain skill set or one that has to make an effort to 'consume the product'. It makes you understand and feel understood as well. It is the precious lifeblood of a master spirit. The further you delve into it, the more it begins to make sense.

It confirms the belief that one book, one pen, one child or one teacher can change the world. It is the axe for a frozen sea.

My own personal experiences in working with this most vibrant mind have been educative and enlightening. I do believe that those who read this book would have a similar sentiment.

I extend my most fervent wishes to Piyushji, not just for this reading, but for the continuation of his effervescent presence and delightful company—a rarity in today's times!

26 August 2015

Amitabh Bachchan

Preface

I can never forget that freezing cold, winter morning in Jaipur when I was five years old, waking up at five to a deep and melodious voice singing, '*Chidiya choon choon karke boli bhor nikal kar aayee kya, bitiya padi bichhona pooche, Amma chai pakiyi kya.*' In English, this verse translates to: 'Little birds are chirping as the sun rises / my little baby, tucked up in her bed, asks, "Mother, is the tea cooked?"'

The voice that rang through the house belonged to my father; the target audience was my mother. The verse was created spontaneously, provoked by my sister asking my mother if the tea was cooked.

Cooked tea? Sounds strange? My father didn't correct my sister, choosing to go with the flow.

Each morning in Jaipur was equally magical, as my father almost serenaded my mother with poetry made up on the spur of the moment, in response to something he had just seen or heard. This morning, the inspiration was my sister's use of the word 'cooked' with 'tea'. It could have been anything else, like birdsong, the weather, smells from the kitchen, the colour of the sky, or the pattering of rain.

This is how the day began for my eight siblings and me. My father's daily dose of childish, impulsive and entertaining verse was our wake-up call. Compare this to the jarring sound of the modern-day alarm clock, and I'll take the cooked tea any day. One by one, as we woke up, we would rush to the kitchen, get a cup of tea and find some room in a corner of our father's quilt for an early morning snuggle and hug. As we sipped on the tea, he would recite poetry peppered with analogies that taught us simple things about life. My mother would be in and out, serving tea continuously, and chipping in with her own creations or with corrections to father's verse if she believed that he had got it wrong.

As I think back on those wonderful mornings, I feel that these were my kindergarten lessons in communication. Whatever you say, say it with respect for the audience, say it in a context that the audience can understand, say it spontaneously, say it without fear, say it not to intimidate or frighten, but to delight.

Whatever you say, say it with respect for the audience, say it in a context that the audience can understand, say it spontaneously, say it without fear, say it not to intimidate or frighten, but to delight.

All through my career, whenever I am in need of inspiration, I transport myself back in time to that cold Jaipur winter morning, and to the same rhyme about the cooked tea.

It's my rhyme that I share with you in this book. I hope you enjoy it, and find your own rhyme. The special rhyme that stays with you, the special rhyme that takes you to a special place, the special rhyme that inspires you with energy, optimism and joy.

1

EVERYONE AND EVERYTHING AROUND YOU IS A TEACHER

1

I Was Born in a Creative Factory

Every creative person is the result of the environment in which he or she was brought up. All that you imbibed right from the age of one or two, the people that you are associated with, family, friends, the house help, everyone makes you what you are.

My family has been the core of my existence. It was a family of eleven people—my parents, my seven elder sisters, my younger brother and me. Yes, I know what you are thinking. We could indeed have formed our own cricket team. My late father, Indra Narayan Pandey, who retired as a government servant, played a significant role in my development as a creative person. He, too, was one. He was a gifted artist, doing theatre, participating in debates and writing poetry. Unfortunately, he couldn't pursue the arts because he had a family to look after. While he was a reasonably accomplished artist, he was a very poor entrepreneur, having run a small trading business and lost his entire investment in it. Forced to work to sustain the family, he took a government job. In addition, he used to teach English to the royalty of Jodhpur to stretch his income. He was an extremely well-read man with a love for both English and Hindi literature. If that wasn't enough, he embraced great poetry, as a result of which our house regularly hosted poetry recitals.

Just being in the house, around my father, I became a lover of poetry. What my father could not actualize with regard to his own creative talents, he practised them with his children. He spent a lot of time preparing me for elocution contests, poetry recitals and competitions, correcting my intonations and nuances, as well as underlining words to bring out the feelings.

One such training session was a total disaster. It was a school elocution contest and he was to prepare me for the finals. He chose a poem called '*Meera ka Vishpan*'. This is the story of Meera, the disciple of Lord Krishna, and how she was forced into drinking poison to kill herself. It was wonderful poetry, but really, really heavy in its language and complex to understand. As a seven-year-old, I mugged it up and in a full auditorium, Ravindra Ranga Manch in Jaipur, with about 700–800 students, parents and special invitees, I stood up and recited this poem. I lost. I lost because the poetry was so heavy that it went not only over the heads of the audience and the teachers, but also over the heads of the judges.

I think I got an elementary lesson of understanding target audiences that day. I went back home and shared with my father what had happened that day. I explained how I performed, how I had my delivery and emphases correct, and so on. My father heard me out and admitted that he had got the choice of the poem wrong. He assured me that he would get the selection right the next time and prepare me such that I won.

I was selected from my class for the next recitation contest. This time, my father chose a poem that was a political satire. The poem began, '*Idhar bhi gaddhe hain, udhar bhi gaddhe hain, jidhar dekhta hoon, gaddhe hi gaddhe hain*' (There are donkeys on my left, there are donkeys on my right, wherever I look there are donkeys everywhere). My father's training required me to first point to one half of the audience (idhar bhi gaddhe hain), then to the other half (udhar be gaddhe hain), and so on. By the time I had completed the first stanza, the audience was in splits. I won the gold medal for the performance.

My father had learnt from the experience, and he knew that he had got the targeting correct this time. No more of the heavy 'Meera ka Vishpan' kind of poem in recitation contests; it would be light, entertaining poetry. For the next big contest, he chose a poem called '*Itihaas ka Parcha*'. It was a poem about a student appearing for his history exam. The student had completely skipped preparing for the exam and was praying to God for a solution. He speaks to God, and God gives him the licence to make up the answers. The student does so, with disastrous results. The audience was in raptures, literally rolling in the aisles.

These two victories gave me the confidence that I carry with me till today as far as public speaking is concerned. Today, I am invited to speak at various forums to address audiences of varying sizes and profiles, and I have no fear, no stage fright. More importantly, I am careful about selecting the content for a speech, be it for a pitch or a client meeting, always ensuring that what I say brings a smile to the recipients.

*

My mother, Bhagwati Pandey, was actually the creative director of the 'factory' and the biggest inspiration to all of us. She was educated only up to Class VIII, was married off at eighteen and came to Jodhpur to live with my father. When my father bought her the first gift, she ran up to her room, hugely excited to open it. She expected some jewellery or a sari. She opened the packet and found two books of Hindi literature. She was so disappointed that she cried all night. I have captured this incident in a story titled 'Two Books and a Life' that I wrote about my mother in a magazine.

From then on, Bhagwati read those books and many more. She went on to read almost everything that she could lay her hands on. Somewhere along the way she decided that her children ought to excel at the arts and culture. With the support of my father, she educated each one of us to the best of our ability. Isn't it remarkable that an 'eighth-class-pass' girl went on to actually teach her daughters when they were doing their master's?

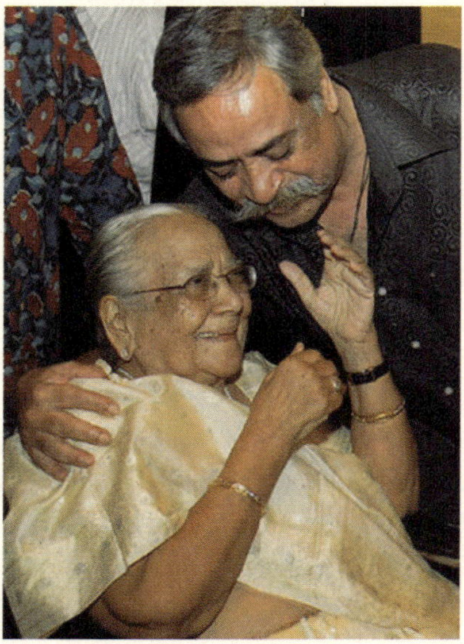

With my mother, the biggest inspiration for the entire family.

She treated her children like a good creative director treats his or her ideas, nurturing and protecting them day in and day out. She stood against family and society, and refused to marry off her daughters at eighteen. One of my sisters, Rama, went to study film in Holland in the seventies. It must have been a nightmare for my mom to explain this to relatives and neighbours. She helped each of her ideas grow and she held them closely bound like Fevicol! Yes, that is my name for my mother. I call her Fevicol because she held us all together. Even as an eighty-nine-year-old, she was the first to wish anyone a 'happy birthday' or a 'happy anniversary'. She would also remind all others about the day and ensure that we wished each other. All such dates, details and information were stored in her blue diary.

Just being in the house, thanks to my mother, I became a lover of books, of reading as well as writing.

My eldest sister, the late Hemlata, had two PhDs, of which one was in Hindi. She was my Hindi teacher, my educator and my librarian. Each time I wrote in Hindi, each time I needed help, I would run up to her with questions: 'What is the meaning of this word? Where did this come from? What are its origins?' She would know the answers, and I would get to learn. Later, as I embarked on a career in advertising, my education in Hindi continued, except it was now on the phone.

Just being in the house, with my sister, I became a lover of Hindi.

My second sister, Sudha, is an MA in English literature, the self-appointed doctor of the family because of her great interest in Ayurveda (even now, she surreptitiously instructs my cook to serve me all kinds of concoctions, and fruit and vegetable juices), and is an accomplished sitar player. She is also the de facto family priest—it sometimes seems that half her day goes into praying for the rest of the family.

Just being in the house, thanks to my sister, I gained an appreciation for music and exposure to Ayurveda.

My third sister, the late Uma, a fabulous singer, cook, tailor, knitter, stylist and disciplinarian was my mother's deputy. She was a surrogate mother to all siblings, younger or older! She had that licence from my mother. Her greatest contribution to our creative factory being recognized today has been in the form of her son Abhijit Awasthi, a celebrated creative leader (till recently, NCD—National Creative Director—of Ogilvy India) and daughter Ashima (Senior Creative Director, BBC Worldwide). It is commendable that both the brother and sister were jury members at the Cannes Advertising Festival 2015.

My fourth sister, Rama, who worked with the BBC for nine years, is an actress, writer, director and producer. She was my teacher of mythology and history, oratory and theatre. She now writes children's books and distributes them in schools. I don't think she earns any money from her writing; she writes because she feels the need to share. She also creates non-fiction TV shows focusing on subjects ranging from history to how Muslim women in India are fighting adverse situations.

Sitting on ground (from L–R)*: Swati Pai, Ashima Awasthi, Tavishi Pandey, Aayushman Pandey, Kavita Awasthi. Sitting on chairs* (from L–R)*: Rama Pandey, Sudha Bajpai, Hemlata Mishra, Bhagwati Pandey, Snehlata Mishra, Ajay Awasthi. Standing in third row* (from L–R)*: Nita Joshi, Deepa Dixit, Ila Arun, Tripti Pandey, Gayatri Pandey. Standing on toes* (from L–R)*: Abhijit Awasthi, Nishant Dixit, Nihar Saqib, Prasoon Pandey, Piyush Pandey.*

Just being in the house, thanks to my sister, I was exposed to both mythology and history.

I was not the first person in the family who got into advertising. It was my sister Ila, now known as Ila Arun.

Ila started a company called Ila Arun Publicity in the early 1970s, making radio jingles for local banks, shops, locks, soaps, agarbattis and other brands from Jaipur that wanted to advertise on Vividh Bharati which had just gone commercial.

Not only was she the first among my siblings to be in the business, my first income from this business came from Ila who used to pay me Rs 50 (less than 1 US$ today) to do voice-over for her jingles.

Ila is a self-taught and self-trained folk singer who kept the house alive with her robust singing and percussion accompaniment on wooden doors and tables. She went on to become the voice of folk singing in Bollywood, a voice and style that inspired hundreds of folk singers in India. A multifaceted personality—film actor, writer, stage performer—she is probably the most famous of all of us today. In fact, she lent her voice to a song in the Oscar-winning film, *Slumdog Millionaire*.

To me, she is the family's music director and theatre expert. Above all, I wouldn't be in advertising if she had not given me a room to stay when I joined the profession in Bombay in 1982.

That brings me to the art director and doctor amongst us. An accomplished doctor in the US, Deepa used to spend as much time on her painting as she did on her medical studies. She was a silent inspiration to the family's art appreciation leanings. Today, if you visit her clinic in Michigan you would think that you got a free trip to an art gallery.

The youngest of my sisters is Tripti, a tourism professional of international acclaim, and a writer (with four published books). She is also the unofficial ambassador of the Rajasthan state; ask the bureaucracy, it would disagree, but ask many tourists, they would vociferously agree. All of us in the family talk about knowing Rajasthan, and all of us run to Tripti when we want to know more or need something done in Rajasthan.

Every creative unit needs to look after its founders, and that is what Tripti has done for decades—looking after the well-being of my parents by being with them in Jaipur, while all of us were pursuing our careers in different parts of the world.

Prasoon Pandey, my brother, is probably a bigger name in advertising than me, because he is of great value to all the advertising agencies and brands in India, unlike me, working with only Ogilvy brands. Public memory is short; most people will not remember that he made a mark internationally long before I did, when Ad Age named him in a list of the Top 25 directors in the world.

Prasoon is certainly more multifaceted than I am. He is an accomplished writer, creative director and a film director, starting with a film that he both wrote and directed for Bajaj Sunny. After this, there was no stopping him, with his film for Sony Ericsson (which, as I say elsewhere in this book, was my idea, but written and shot by Prasoon) winning silver at Cannes. At this stage, I had not yet won a metal at Cannes.

I've had the bizarre experience, many times, when my competitors have called me to get me to use my 'influence' as a brother to get Prasoon to agree to find the time to work on a film for them. It gets worse; there are clients who refuse to work with anyone except Prasoon.

Take Fevicol, for example. If I wrote a script that I believed would suit another director better, Pidilite would have nothing of it. They insist on working with Prasoon as he gives them confidence and comfort.

He does this with many clients. This is not just because of his writing and directing skills, but also because of another great skill: his understanding of music. To understand what music can do, watch the Fevicol bus film, first with the volume turned to mute and then with the volume turned up. Music directors speak to me of the interplay between Prasoon and them which results in magical music output. Prasoon is a trained designer, too, who has a fantastic sense of design and film, not to speak of music, and all bolstered by his intense interest in Indian culture.

In a way, he has changed the way Indian ads look, bringing in 'raw' faces, thanks to his manic interest in perfect casting. Whether it's the Fevikwik fisherman film or the M-Seal Will film or the Bajaj Sunny one, he spends time finding actors who fit his script to a T—and then spends time with them to get them to perform at their best.

Prasoon is my brother, but I'll still say it. He's probably the best storyteller in the advertising industry that India has ever seen. When one tries to analyse why this is so, it's probably because that's how he views his role. He wants to partner with the creative team from the advertising agency at the script stage itself, allowing more exchanges of thoughts and ideas as a partner and not as an external vendor or solution provider.

In the Fevikwik fisherman film, casting is everything.

Most importantly, as he does with me, he can help the creative director visualize how the consumer will view the film that we're discussing at the script stage.

When I work with Prasoon, he is the partner that I can trust 100 per cent. In many ways, he is responsible for half of what I am. How would the Fevicol films that I've done have looked without Prasoon's inputs? How would my career have ended up without Prasoon's inputs?

Finally, I come to my secret creative director, Nita. Nita came into my life a little late. We got married in 2000 after a courtship that was shorter than six months. At that point, she was vice president at Ogilvy, heading Client Servicing. When I was promoted as chairman, Nita quit, believing that it would be inappropriate for her to carry on while being married to me.

It was when she quit that she discovered that there was a creative director in her which was waiting to be discovered. She explored the arts, electing to do a course in mosaic in a renowned studio in Italy as a hobby. The hobby consumed her, and, in some time, she had a large enough body of work to have her own exhibition. More than half the exhibited pieces were sold, and Nita, the creative director, was established.

From this point on, Nita was my sounding board on every single idea. She listens to my ideas patiently and critiques them dispassionately. She would tell me if she loved an idea—and, with the same candidness, tell me if she hated one. She's also been an inspiration for ideas. The famous campaign for Ponds' Cold Cream, 'Googly Woogly Woosh', was a direct lift from what Nita did one day in a romantic moment, grabbing hold of my cheeks and saying, 'Googly Woogly Woosh'. The campaign ran for ten years!

Later, she discovered the architect and the designer in her—as I did too. We were looking to buy a flat to live in, in Bombay, and Nita wanted me to check out a flat in Shivaji Park. Shivaji Park? I had worked my way up from a small flat in the western suburbs of Andheri to Khar to Malabar Hill, and she wanted us to live in Shivaji Park?

This Ponds' film was inspired by Nita, my wife.

Bullied by her, I went to see the flat. It was just as I had feared—a dingy hole in the wall. I was aghast. But Nita described, in vivid detail, what she would do to the flat, to the drawing room, to the bedrooms, to the loos, to the terrace. Her conviction in her own abilities and her enthusiasm caused me to succumb.

Today, when someone comes to the flat for the first time, he or she is stunned, asking me how on earth I discovered it. That's when I tell them that I had nothing to do with it. The flat was all Nita's doing; her imagination, her vision and, most importantly, her ability to work with masons, carpenters and painters to transform her dream into what we see today.

This was just the beginning of her new life as a creative genius. After this, she designed the Ogilvy office in Bombay which looks as far from a corporate office as one can imagine. She identified a house for us to buy in Goa, and redesigned every inch of it.

Today, as a business, she helps design houses in Goa. During the course of her surfing the Net, she becomes a curator for me, sharing videos and articles that she believes would be of interest and value to me. I am all but illiterate when it comes to technology in general and the computer in particular, so Nita becomes my eyes and ears for all things good on the Net. God knows how many campaign ideas have been sparked by something that Nita drew my attention to. She knows me inside out, she knows what will inspire me, and she makes it a point to show me all those things which I am incapable of seeing on my own.

Nita is the successful creative director behind the successful creative director. There is a management lesson to be learnt from looking at how Nita has dealt with my family, the large, dominating Rajasthani family full of opinionated, strong-willed people. We're very different from the average Maharashtrian family (which Nita was born in), being loud, boisterous and emotional, ready to cry at the drop of a hat. With all the cultural differences, she merged into my family without making any compromises on what she believed was right or proper. Relationships are tough to forge and maintain. The ultimate certification is in the rapport she shared with my mother. With the age difference, my mother could easily have been Nita's grandmother; yet, Nita built a relationship that resembled a friendship of peers. My mother and Nita could say whatever they wanted to each other.

I try to understand how Nita managed to achieve this closeness with every single member of the family. The answer is simple: she did not look at how different they were; she looked for what was common. That's the management lesson.

I was lucky to have a large family. This does not mean that everyone should have a large family. Everyone doesn't. What I mean is, we need to build a community of friends or people around us who possess different talents. People who we can learn from. No matter what their area of expertise. People whose criticisms are constructive. People whose appreciation is genuine. They could be anybody around us. All we need is to reach out. If you add value to their lives they will do it to you too.

As for me, since we siblings are friends, we speak to each other as often as we can. Many of the calls might be to just say hello to each other, but many of the calls are work related for the simple reason that there is so much overlap in the things that we do. I would imagine that, on an average day, I receive at least five calls from my siblings, whether from Boston or Jaipur or Bhopal or Delhi or here in Bombay—and there would be another five that I make.

We need to build a community of friends or people around us who possess different talents.

It's not just the phone calls—we try to meet each other as often as we can. We find excuses to meet—a wedding, a birthday, an anniversary, a religious or cultural celebration; each is an excuse to meet. More than that, each is an opportunity to talk to each other, to discuss what is happening personally and professionally, to bounce off ideas and thoughts.

My family has been my Google. If I had a question, my family had the answers. As with Google, one had to know where to look. Do I ask Ila? Tripti? Prasoon? Nita? Once I figure that out, the answer comes easily.

I'll share a simple thought from Indian literature, which goes, '*Kasturi kundal basey, mrig dhundhey van maahi.*' The line describes the behaviour of the musk deer. The deer doesn't realize that the musk it smells is in its own body, and runs around the jungle searching for the source.

We're like the musk deer, going far and wide for answers and solutions when, in all likelihood, they're right next to us.

When you have a question, look for answers in your own personal Google—your family and friends. Your immediate circle is an extraordinary repository of information, and a lot of that information is not available on Google. Your personal Google would have opinions, anecdotes, insights and history that you cannot even think of finding in the digital Google. I'm fortunate to have been born in a large family, but most of you are likely to be born in a smaller family. Find and create an extended family. Your uncles and aunts, your nephews and nieces, your neighbour. All of them, put together, form a formidable Google that you can turn to.

My own Google extended beyond my immediate family. My mother has five sisters, each of whom had children. That meant a lot of travel and a lot of visitors—a treasure trove of conversations and knowledge. And trivia.

Sometimes I get answers to questions that I didn't even ask. I have never asked anyone how stuffed bhindis are made, but I know exactly how. I know because of my Google—which is more than the flat, unidimensional screen you see. I've heard everything about stuffed bhindi; how the bhindi needs to be washed and cut, what ingredients are required for the stuffing, how much oil is required, what colour the bhindi should be before you turn off the stove. For all those who know cooking, this may seem like useless trivia. But that's the beauty of trivia—you never know when it will come in handy. When I was invited to Mr Bachchan's sixty-ninth birthday, I had no clue what to give him. That's when some bells rang. Mr Bachchan loved bhindi, and I knew how to cook a wonderful bhindi dish. That was that; I cooked it and took it across—and he loved it. That's precisely the beauty of trivia. What is trivia today can be transformed into spectacular insight tomorrow. Perhaps, if I was in another mood, it would have been stuffed bhindi instead of dal in the Fortune Cooking Oil ad film. From the sublime to the ridiculous, you see all in your own Google.

The personal Google becomes infinitely more powerful when you add more 'sources'. So, add your friends. I have had the good fortune of having some wonderful friends. Some of these relationships are predictable and some very strange. Who can explain why or how Vijay Krishna, who I first met when we were in Class VI, became one of the greatest friends I have ever had? Vijay was a scholar and topped almost every exam that he wrote while I was a backbencher, the kind of student teachers dread. He cared nothing for sports, for me, sports, particularly cricket, was everything.

To underline the contrast, Vijay went on to teach at Harvard Business School. My father often said to me, referring to Vijay, 'This is the kind of boy you should be.'

At the same time, the sports-hating Vijay would be consumed by my success at sports. The committed-to-education Vijay, when at the Delhi School of Economics, would bunk classes, pick up his fiancé, and come to watch me play cricket for St. Stephen's. And whatever sport I took part in, he wanted me to win. He would watch and cheer, and encourage me. (He even lent me his US-made swimming trunks for every swimming competition I took part in because he thought that they would give me an edge.)

However, the biggest support I got from Vijay was in getting into St. Stephen's College after school. Having done poorly at school, I didn't have a hope in hell. No one believed that I could—except for Vijay. Miraculously, I was accepted at St. Stephen's College in the Bachelor of Arts programme. Once in, it was Vijay who reminded me that we (he and I) had made a commitment to my parents that I would work hard and excel in college. He insisted that I did all my studies, revisions and assignments in his room. He made everything sound simple. If I could spend the whole year playing cricket, why couldn't I spend sixteen hours a day in the month preceding the examinations in studying? Vijay kept on till I took him seriously, and took him on. I went on to top the university in the first year. Encouraged by the success, I continued to study hard, and won scholarships each year thereon.

This is all due to Vijay Krishna, with whom, seemingly, I had nothing in common.

That's a lesson you could learn (I learnt it in hindsight). There is a strange, powerful chemistry between people who seem completely dissimilar; so, do not reject those who you think have nothing in common with you. Perhaps, you should build a relationship because there is nothing in common, as in the case of Vijay and me.

My Google became more powerful, with Vijay's inputs added to it. Not just Vijay's; his father's as well. His father, Dr Raj Krishna, an eminent economist, took me under his wings, and would often take Vijay and me to the movies. Watching films was fun, but it was in the conversations and laughter that our relationship grew. What this family saw in me I have no clue. Perhaps, I shouldn't look for one. The only answer is there was, patently, a wonderful human chemistry between all of us.

Human chemistry is extremely important in the business of communication. Creating communication requires diverse sets of people to come together, have conversations, debates and arguments—all towards the greater cause of creating great work. Otherwise, would I ever have sought out Vijay to help me plan my life? Vijay was nothing like me, but has contributed so much to what I am today.

Sometimes it's good to have a ghost as a friend. I'm referring to my friend Anil Kumar, popularly known as Bhoot (Ghost). Anil was rechristened Bhoot when we were in Class II—and his favourite pastime was to frighten the daylights out of the Class I students at night.

Bhoot and I have been friends now for more than fifty years, including being classmates from Class I till the time we were done with our MA final.

Bhoot is a great adventurer. He has been a farmer, an owner of a dairy and a tea planter. The only constant has been his passion for birdwatching. He calls a spade a spade, and has a complete disregard for theory and has no desire to conform. His basic philosophy in life is to get on with it with a smile. Has

Bhoot's unusual way of life influenced some of my work and some of my attitude? Perhaps the answer is 'yes'.

While I write this book, a new factory is rapidly taking shape which includes the children of my siblings and their spouses. There is a doctor-cum-Odissi (Indian classical) dancer, a doctor-cum-birdwatcher, an ex-country head of HBO, a marketing professional of a multinational, a chemistry professor-cum-painter (chemistry helps!), an ad agency owner with a wife who has multiple artistic achievements, an advertising heavyweight and a wife who is a planner, a BBC documentary creative director and a husband who is an internationally awarded animator, a Disney promo producer, an actress–designer and a husband who is a music director of international repute, a lawyer (wish I had one) and a husband who is an eye surgeon to ensure you see your consumer right, an assistant ad film director who already has a New York Festivals statue, a nephew who is hell-bent on proving that at least one from the family can create a successful start-up, and finally, a liberal arts student to ensure that creativity stays fresh and young.

This huge lot doesn't live together, but they have a dangerous weapon—a WhatsApp group called PANDEYMONIUM, which is seriously active. Competitors, beware! Incidentally, here is where I got the inspiration for the title of the book. Again, my personal Google helped.

My family and friends will keep returning in this book, as and when they play a role in what I did. So often, there is no way that their contribution could have been anticipated. That's the beauty of family and friends. You are close to them because they are family and friends. And because they are close to you, they will influence you. They will inspire you, they will enrich you, they will help you become what you finally do become.

2

Life Is a Game of Cricket

It's only with the benefit of hindsight that one can begin to define all one's influences. While there is no doubt that my family and the environment that I grew up in has proved to be the greatest influence in my career as an advertising professional, the game of cricket is a close second.

One remembers great teachers with fondness and gratitude, and of all the teachers I have had, the game of cricket is the one teacher I remember the most. Perhaps it's because I spent the most time with, and interacted most with, Cricket Sir. While at school or in college, my priority was always cricket over the classroom.

Way back in the seventies, when my love affair with cricket began, cricket wasn't the leading sport in India—it was hockey. Today, cricket is the great binding agent in India after Bollywood, and, without realizing that, I was slowly and relentlessly acquiring knowledge of the sport which would end up capturing the imagination of men, women and children in India, the sport that brands would have to embrace to connect to their target audiences, the sport that would give India more heroes and brand ambassadors than any other, the sport which would dominate the front pages of newspapers, and prime time on news television, the sport that would be the first sport to have TV channels dedicated solely to it.

Cricket would become a category—and I would become a category expert.

Heady cricketing days (from L–R)*: Amrit Mathur, Arun Lal, myself and Kirti Azad.*

From the days, over fifty years ago, that I seemed to irresponsibly prioritize cricket over academics, it's been an extraordinary journey to where I've reached today as chairman of Ogilvy, the largest advertising agency in India. And much of it is due to cricket.

It was due to my relative success at cricket that I got to travel the length and breadth of India, participating in various tournaments, seeing an India which most young men my age didn't have the opportunity to do. Travel exposed me to various cultures, sounds, colours, music, food and languages. Travel exposed me to the spectacular variety of terrains, the variety of villages, towns and cities that form India.

Cricket taught me how to be a player in a team; it taught me how to accept both defeat and victory alike. The longer form taught me patience, it taught me how to anticipate developments, and form strategies. Cricket also taught me how to be led, and, later, to lead. Cricket helped me meet, literally, hundreds of people, many of whom would turn out to be mentors in my life.

This was the curriculum that fate designed for me—and it could well be a curriculum created for an advanced course in advertising.

Cricket found a way into many brands that I worked on.

Cricket is everything in this Cadbury Dairy Milk ad.

Cricket seemed to intrude into all aspects of my professional life even as I embarked on a career in advertising. It first made an entry into the communication that I created in a television commercial for Cadbury Dairy Milk, when a girl runs on to the field during the game to celebrate her friend's achievement. Cricket has, since then, made regular and meaningful appearances in my work, the latest being the animated television commercials for the BJP for their Lok Sabha election campaign in 2014.

These, however, pale into insignificance when compared to Ogilvy's now famous association with the Indian Premier League (IPL).

In the mid-nineties, when Lalit Modi was running Modi Entertainment Networks and had a joint venture with Walt Disney Pictures, I, along with my friends Arun Lal and Amrit Mathur, met him with a concept which was almost identical to the IPL we see today.

Lalit Modi approached the Board of Control for Cricket in India (BCCI) with our concept note, and the BCCI summarily threw it out, perhaps as a result of the politics and power games of the time. A similar concept, the Indian Cricket League (ICL), was created by Zee TV later, but ended up as a failure.

As the ICL came a cropper, Lalit Modi became an official of the Rajasthan Cricket Association (RCA) and subsequently found his way to a position of power in the BCCI. That's when he said to me, 'Let's pull out the concept again.' The original concept was then updated, made relevant, and it is the IPL that you know today.

Even as Arun, Amrit and I were delighted, there was criticism in the media that the IPL was nothing but a rehashed, improved version of the ICL, and that there was nothing original about it. As in advertising, being accused of copying someone else's idea is rankling, to say the least, and I was seething at the reports. In the media, however, it was Lalit Modi being accused of copying, not Arun, Amrit and myself. So, it was an aggressive, angry and slighted Lalit Modi who wrote in an article that the concept of the IPL was written—by Piyush Pandey, Arun Lal and Amrit Mathur—years before the ICL was born.

Soon, Modi and the BCCI put the accusations behind them and moved ahead with complete conviction to create a tournament that would pit city against city, that would be played under lights, that would embrace young and old and male and female fans alike, and that would be both carnival and cricket. In the first presentation that we made to the BCCI, I wrote a line which said, 'Carnival outside the boundary line, pure cricket inside.' That's what the IPL became.

Learning from Cricket

We (St. Stephen's) were playing a very important game. It was the Delhi University inter-college final traditionally fought between St. Stephen's and Hindu College every year. It was a five-day game, a format that I had never played before. I was only in my second year then, and I watched anxiously as my seniors, and our fantastic batting line-up, failed. On day one, before lunch, we had 53 runs on the board and the sixth wicket fell. The sixth dismissal was that of my dear friend Arun Lal who had scored 44 of those 53 runs. As he was returning to the pavilion and I was going in to bat, we exchanged a few words. 'You know what, 53 for 6 is a huge problem for ordinary people. It is an opportunity of a lifetime for somebody who wants to be great,' he said. I scored 71 runs that day. Arun taught me to always remember that in adversity lies an opportunity. If I had gone in to bat at 500 for 2 and scored a century, few would have noticed or remembered. But those who saw me, a young man in the second year, score 71 after coming in at 53 for 6 noticed and remembered me.

When times are tough, the 53 for 6 comes to mind. And I'm determined to score another 71.

Arun has taught me so much; dealing with tough times is just one of them.

And the rest is history.

For Ogilvy, however, it wasn't all smooth sailing. When Ogilvy was invited to pitch for the IPL account, there was a miscommunication that led to a meeting at which the BCCI expected us to present creative work—but we had gone with just a presentation of our agency's credentials. After checking the mail trail and acknowledging that there was a lack of clarity in the communication, they gave us the opportunity to present again but within forty-eight hours.

Carnival outside the boundary, pure cricket inside. That's what the IPL has become.

In those forty-eight hours, we were able to put together the Karmayudh theme and present the creative, and were fortunately awarded the account. Winning the IPL account was just the beginning—we also won the accounts for three of the eight IPL teams, Rajasthan Royals, Mumbai Indians and Deccan Chargers.

In the conventional world of advertising, working for the IPL and for three IPL teams would have been unthinkable as it would have been seen as working for four brands in the same category. We managed to convince the three teams that, far from being in conflict with each other, all the teams needed to work with the IPL to create a larger brand, and that all the teams participating in the IPL had a common purpose. The larger and more valuable the IPL brand became, the larger and more valuable each team brand would become.

There are times in advertising when there is no direct conflict and yet people try and see conflicts. Clients introduce grandfather clauses around conflicts that they seem to see. For example, we might be told that if we handled a toothpaste brand, we couldn't work on another company's toothbrush account. Where is the conflict? Toothbrushes and toothpaste are complementary to each other; the better one does, the better it is for the other.

So it was with the IPL. If one team could be seen as a toothbrush, another could be a toothpaste.

The IPL is a rare example of a huge brand being created and becoming commercially successful in the first year itself. Ogilvy has been continuously and deeply associated with the IPL and with some of the teams since its inception, helping the IPL achieve the goal of being embraced by all ages, by both genders, and by the rich and poor alike.

Ogilvy has more involvement with the IPL, and earns more revenue from it than from any other agency. It's because we know cricket as a category, and all that it entails, better than any other agency.

So, does that mean that one had to be as passionate about cricket as I have been to understand the category and create cricket-based communication? Not necessarily.

One doesn't have to know how to wear a sanitary napkin to sell one. However, if you are passionate about a category, it helps. It's my passion for cricket that perhaps comes through during presentations, discussions and negotiations. To be passionate about a category that one works on is imperative.

If you can read David Ogilvy or Bill Bernbach and every word that has been written by advertising greats, so can anyone else. However, one has to go beyond the reading. Clients know that all creative partners of similar size are similar as far as their abilities and infrastructure are concerned. When evaluating an agency partner, clients want to see how differently each interprets a brief and then how passionate an agency is about the category and the brand. The marketer will ask: 'Which agency seems excited about my brand?' 'Which agency gives me the feeling that the team across the table from me is not an agency, but an extension of my own team?'

One doesn't have to know how to wear a sanitary napkin to sell one.

It's the passion and the involvement that counts in the end. Real passion and real involvement, not pretended and play-acted. Ogilvy's passion for cricket is real. That's perhaps why, a few years after the IPL began, we were invited by the BCCI to help them win the rights to host the ICC World Cup in the Indian subcontinent, even as it seemed, as was being reported in various media, that it was all but awarded to the Australia–New Zealand combine.

Lalit Modi and the BCCI insisted that no match was over till the last over was bowled, and challenged us to prepare a bid that would help the BCCI win. In monetary terms, there couldn't be much to differentiate the BCCI bid from the Australia–New Zealand one. We had to create communication that would demonstrate that the Indian bid was better. The Ogilvy team decided to avoid the predictable and expected PowerPoint presentation. Under Sagar Mahabaleshwarkar who headed the team, we designed and printed a coffee-table book with letters from then prime minister Manmohan Singh, some letters from the Sri Lankan cricket board and letters from Pakistan. The book featured great photographs of what cricket meant to the subcontinent, with images of cricket on the streets, cricket in the lanes and bylanes of the three countries, visually underlining what cricket represented to this region. We underlined that while Australia and New Zealand boasted of many popular sports, the subcontinent reserved all its passion for just one sport: cricket.

The bid was a winning one. Our passion won.

By now, we had become the trusted partners of the BCCI—and the success story grew. We then worked with our Sri Lankan partner on the successful bid for the T20 World Cup which was played in Sri Lanka.

Passion won again.

If I think back, it seems impossible for me to separate my professional life from cricket. When I clearly prioritized cricket over my formal school and college education, my late father was far from amused, saying repeatedly to me, 'Stop playing this damned game, because when you become an adult, you will not be able to eat a bat for a meal.'

I wish I could tell him that now I am eating a bat for a meal.

*

There are many occasions when cricket comes into my conversations, both official and unofficial—that's because there is so much learning that I draw from cricket.

Ever since 'traditional' cricket changed, there have been both vehement supporters and critics of every change that we have witnessed. When Packer introduced coloured clothing and night cricket, the traditionalists were all up in arms. The audiences were changing; these new audiences, blue-collar workers from small towns, didn't have the luxury of watching a game that took five days to be completed. The pressure of time, and the advent of colour TV globally, jointly forced the changes that we have seen, first with the One-day format and subsequently with T20.

With the introduction of the new formats, cricket was recharged. Audiences wanted more—and wanted to be entertained every minute that they watched the game on TV, especially in the shorter formats. Non-cricket entertainment was introduced in the shorter-format games. The purists fumed, even as the television audiences surged and stadiums were packed to the rafters.

I still love Test matches. Cricket has not changed; there have been changes to some rules to make the game more exciting. I played my cricket in the years when spinners were the strength of India. The team sometimes playing four spinners—Prasanna, Venkatraghavan, Bishen Singh Bedi and Chandrashekhar—in the same game. This made sense in the days of the five-day Test, when you had a circle of close-in fielders, and if you passed mid-off or mid-on, it was a boundary. With the field placements and the quality of fielding that we see today, four spinners in the same side would be unheard of, even in a Test match.

In recent Test matches outside India, we've seen India play with an all-rounder who can also bowl spin, but with no specialist spinner in the side. Purists may fume, but it is extremely important to accept the changes—and equally important to retain your roots.

Today, while we see fast-food outlets at virtually every street corner, do we stop eating dal, sabzi and chawal at home? We have both, the traditional food and the modern one. Life is not about one or the other, it is about finding the balance. If cricket, one morning in 1966, had changed to the cricket that we know today, all fans, not just the purists, would have rejected the changes and that would have been the end of the game.

So, it is with the business of advertising and communication. The business is not static. Every now and then, we see new opportunities and new challenges. When TV first came to India, we didn't throw away print, radio and outdoor, much as One-day cricket didn't result in the death of Test cricket.

But refusing to embrace the new, refusing to experiment with the new, could result in disastrous consequences. Imagine what would have happened to cricket if Kerry Packer didn't see that the audiences were getting disinterested in the game as it was at that time.

3

Carpenters, Cobblers and Other Creatives

I've forever had a fascination for carpenters and cobblers, spurred largely by the circumstances of growing up in a middle-class family. I don't remember, when I was a young boy, any point in time that the family had enough money to buy ready-made, manufactured, branded furniture straight from a showroom. More importantly, there were so many items of furniture that were thought of as unnecessary then. For example, for many years we had no dining table at home. Traditionally, my mother or my aunt or the maharaj-ji would sit on the floor with an *angithi*, or a sort of contraption, that you used to stoke the coals in the *chullah*. Everyone sat on little platforms, or *paatta*s, and the food was placed in vessels on the floor. The floor was the dining table. As a result, the first dining table coming to my house was a big event for us, evoking a great sense of pride, much like middle-class families experience today when they buy their first Maruti Alto.

I still remember the day when my father decided to get carpenters to make a dining table, which was to be made in the house. Wood was bought by my father at the cheapest possible rate and the carpenters came home to make the furniture. It took a fortnight for the table to be made. My curiosity led me to chat with them, asking them where they came from and where their ancestors came from . . . I learnt that their ancestors were actually artists whose services were used by the maharajahs and the little zamindars of Rajasthan for carving wood. Over the decades, they had transitioned from being artists who created for the rich and the famous to carpenters who made functional furniture. Did we, as a society, respect them less because they were merely providing a necessary service and not creating a work of art? This was a question that haunted me even then. These carpenters, to me, were artists.

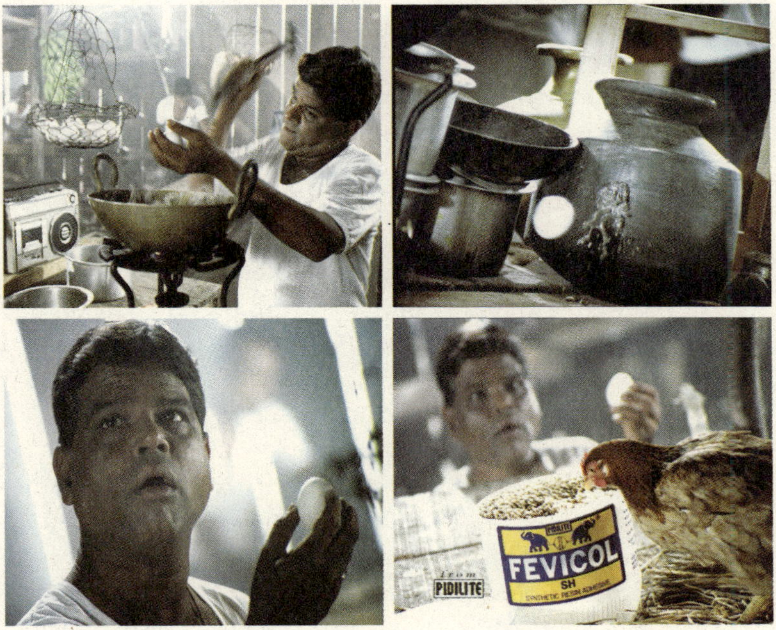

My fascination with carpenters helps immensely on the Fevicol account.

Each time my father commissioned them to make something for the house, I would interact with them and try to understand them and their work better. As with the role that cricket has played in my professional career, my association with these wonderful carpenters would be of help to me and Ogilvy significantly in the future, when we worked on Pidilite's Fevicol account, leading to continuous contact and conversations with them all over again. As a child, my curiosity in carpenters was perhaps because they were the first 'makers' or 'creators' I saw up close; however, from the day I started working on the Fevicol account, the tone of the curiosity changed. Between my childhood and my working on the Fevicol account, my only other connection to carpenters was to *The Carpenters*, the musicians who made difficult evenings more liveable.

Due to the live carpentry sessions that were so much a part of my childhood, and thanks to the consequent exchanges, it was, for me, the easiest thing on earth to relate to these craftsmen, to strike up a conversation and to understand what their concerns, needs and aspirations were. And so it continues till today.

The memory of the conversations that I had with carpenters is a form of research, though not as structured as people might think it to be. The conversations gave me the opportunity to mine them for their thoughts and insights which are much richer than a study that might be conducted by somebody who has never interacted with a carpenter in his life. Each time I see a carpenter I remember that, owing to his roots, deep down resides an artist—an artist whom I hold in great respect. I recognize the artistry when I see a flourish in what would have been a dull and boring piece of furniture, when a carpenter adds a nuance to a bedpost. The more my father demonstrated respect for the craft of the carpenter, the better the furniture would turn out to be.

Now, when I look back, I think to myself, thank God my father didn't have the money to buy ready-made furniture. I would never have been fascinated by these artists—and Ogilvy wouldn't have done great work on the Fevicol brand for decades.

There were more gains for me in my middle-class upbringing. For example, there was the cobbler. When we grew up, no piece of footwear, however old, was discarded till the cobbler gave up. Nothing was thrown away until it was proven to be absolutely of no utility. Extracting the maximum value out of anything was the culture. If a shoe developed a hole, a patch was stitched to give it a new life. If the seams gave way, the cobbler would stitch them again. Worn-out soles were replaced. And if you grew too big for your shoes, they found their way to a smaller sibling, and you, too, would get a hand-me-down from an older one.

Cobblers stretch the lives of footwear—as Fevikwik does.

Cobblers didn't have 'shops'. They sat by the roadside with the tools of their trade, working in full public view. While the cobbler was at work, breathing new life into an old pair of my slippers or shoes, I would watch him, fascinated. As with carpenters, I learnt that cobblers, too, are artists—fantastic artists. You watch a cobbler redo the stitching and then watch how the stiches disappear as he polishes the shoe. He completes the repair job and hands the shoe over, asking you to check that it's comfortable, wanting to know that the nail he's just hammered has embedded well or not.

The whole exercise of getting something repaired by the cobbler was interactive and participatory, full of questions and answers. The cobbler kept probing till he was certain that the job was done well, and that his client found the footwear comfortable. The time spent was not important; he took as much time on a job as was needed to have a satisfied client.

There are many things that I learnt from the cobbler. My common refrain of passion—the desire to do a job as well as it could be done, without bothering about how much more time perfection would need and, finally, the need to see a truly satisfied customer; because only a truly satisfied customer would come back repeatedly.

Only a truly satisfied customer would come back repeatedly.

So, I learnt from the carpenter and the cobbler, but my education didn't end there. I had another teacher, a man who used to repair punctured cycle tyres. Cycles gave us our sense of freedom. The cycle made us mobile, gave us the opportunity to explore new places and spaces. Roads, then, were not what they are today. Indeed, some of the 'roads' were merely paths, strewn with stones and gravel—and punctures were the order of the day. The puncture-repairman would take half an hour on the entire process, first in locating the exact spot of the puncture, then in sanding down the offending area, and finally cutting and attaching a patch to seal the leak. And, as with the carpenter and the cobbler, each visit was a conversation and an education. Similar learnings, too. To strive for complete customer satisfaction, to take as much time as is required to do a thorough job. To be confident that the job is so well done that the customer will come back when he again faces problems.

The carpenter, the cobbler and the puncture-repairman probably didn't do even a year's formal education, let alone finish college or go to a business school. Yet, each of them targeted perfection, and attempted to deliver complete client satisfaction to a point that loyalty is built. All of them were great conversationalists and would have made successful client-facing professionals if fate had been kinder to them. They might be just carpenters, cobblers or puncture-repairmen, but with the fire to be the best carpenters, cobblers or puncture-repairmen in the world.

That's the lesson from these artists that I value the most. To want to be the best in what I do—and do all that it takes to take me there.

4

Heritage on Wheels

When I look back at my childhood, I feel fortunate that I got to see and experience life from very early on. It was literally a 'mobile' training programme. My father used to work with the Rajasthan government's cooperative department. His job involved lending money to farmers as well as collecting it back from them. This meant a lot of travel to remote rural areas of Rajasthan, sometimes to far-flung villages, in a jeep. I travelled with him frequently, regardless of 47°C heat in summer or 3°C chill in winter. We used to stay in government accommodation and eat whatever the villagers ate. I used to play with the kids around while my father would be at work. Little did I realize that I was beginning to appreciate and respect the hard-core Indian way of living. It is not a coincidence that time and again there is a touch of Rajasthan in my work. Early this year, the Maharana Mewar Charitable Foundation awarded me the Haldi Ghati Award. That night I cried as I remembered going to Haldi Ghati with my father as a nine-year-old. During the trip, he had narrated to me how Maharana Pratap had fought a pitched battle here against the Moghuls.

*

I have a tremendous fascination for trains and a deep respect for Indian Railways which I feel is truly the lifeline of our nation.

Trains have been the most critical mode of transport for Indians, particularly for the poor and the middle class. I am thankful to God for being born in a middle-class family; otherwise, I would have missed out on travelling in trains and the most beautiful training programme that life had designed for me.

Our family is originally from Uttar Pradesh and therefore all our relatives lived there. We were probably the only ones in Rajasthan. So, every vacation, my mother used to take all of us to visit her mother, brothers, sisters and dozens of cousins. It was a time we looked forward to. The magic of the unreserved third-class compartment. The joy of reaching the station a few hours early to occupy the berths. The thrill of creating extra berths by joining trunks (there were no suitcases in our house). Jumping around on the upper berths as if we were monkeys on a tree. Somehow, the same food that we ate at home, tasted better in a train.

The travel would last at least twenty-four hours and during the journey you met other families. The thing about such travels is that you make new friends. You share food as if you have known each other for a long time. People bare their souls to each other like they wouldn't with their family and friends. Perhaps this confidence to confide comes from the fact that they will probably not meet the fellow passenger again in their lives and there is no risk of the conversation reaching those that you have talked about. These train journeys are full of great stories. Stories about different people. Stories that have made my advertising skills richer. You can see a glimpse of this in the television commercial of SBI Life where two elder sisters are travelling in a train to meet their kid brother who is only seventy-five years old!

Trains and third-class compartments continued to be a part of my life beyond these trips with my family. As I grew up, I was turning out to be a competent swimmer and cricketer. This meant more travel. Most schools and sporting associations had little money, which entailed more third-class unreserved compartments. And since mom was not on the train, the journeys became more adventurous. We would get off at every station, run to the shop outside to buy snacks (sometimes, beer) and run back to chase and board a moving train.

Great memories: The lifeline of India, Indian Railways.

Playing professional cricket made the train journey longer. During schooldays, it was just the Hindi belt—Rajasthan to Uttar Pradesh. Now it covered national terrain. We used to travel across the country from Kashmir to Kanyakumari. The journeys sometimes were more than forty-eight hours long. En route, the topography changed, languages changed, people and culture changed. And the food in the train changed. On a single journey, the vendor's chant changed from 'Chai Samosa, Chai Chai!' to 'Idli, Vada, Bonda, Upma, Coffee, Coffee!' I was beginning to see a new India and loving it with each journey.

Chatting with all kinds of people has always been very enjoyable for me. What began as making fun of other accents and cultures soon turned into appreciation. I was absorbing, learning without knowing, and yet wanting more of it. The training programme thus kept chugging along.

Once we were travelling from New Delhi to Mysore city for a cricket tournament. It was a very long journey. Delhi to Madras, Madras to Bangalore and then overnight from Bangalore to Mysore city. At Bangalore, my friend, Arun Lal, asked me, 'Have you ever travelled in an engine?' I said no, but I would like to. Arun's father, the late Mr Jagdish Lal (an eminent cricketer in his days) was a senior official of the Indian Railways. Arun met up with the stationmaster and we were unofficially allowed to travel in the engine. I will never forget that wonderful overnight journey in a steam engine. We spent the night helping the driver shovel coal into the furnace. He, in turn, would heat up tea in his aluminium kettle on the furnace and serve us. We chatted about his life and learnt about things like engines, mechanics and engineering that we didn't have a clue about. In the morning, we were in Mysore, faces black with coal, but minds enlightened like never before.

You might wonder why I am sharing the train stories with you. These are for you to read between the lines. For the younger minds, I want to share these stories for them to consider human interactions and their added value to our communication capabilities.

Apart from human beings and cargo, the railways transported the most valuable thing in our lives. It carried communication, or should I say, it carried the Indian Postal Service. Another great service that I salute each time I pass a post office. I doubt if Mahatma Gandhi would have been able to communicate to the entire nation had it not been for post and telegraph. You think email liberates your mind. I think the Indian Postal Service liberated a nation!

My payback time came for both the railways and postal service later on in life. In the nineties, I got the opportunity to do a campaign for India Post. Therein, beyond the call of delivering letters, I saluted the postman and his humanity. They not only deliver letters, but even read them out to those who can't read. Remember, to date 960 million Indians are not on email and 0.8 billion people don't have a mobile.

When my ancestors came to Rajasthan, they got a contract from the postal department to deliver letters to remote rural areas using camels because the train didn't reach everywhere. Today, I feel proud that the signage for India Post that you see around the country is designed by my colleagues at Ogilvy and me.

Working on India Post was a way to pay back.

The railways also gave me an opportunity to pay back a bit. I say 'a bit' because I'd got a lot more from it. A couple of weeks before the Commonwealth Games of 2010, I got a call from the railway board that they needed a film to run during the Games. The Indian Railways was co-sponsor and did a lot of free commercial time on Doordarshan, but they didn't have a film to run. Nor did they have ample time to make one. They asked me, 'Can you make it happen?' 'Yes, I owe my career to you . . .' was my reply. I roped in Prakash Varma (Nirvana) and we pulled off magical stuff within days.

You think email liberates your mind. I think the Indian Postal Service liberated a nation!

The film shows a human train running across Calcutta, and had a sign-off: The Magic of Indian Railways or *Desh ka Mel, Bharatiya Rail*. And actual magic happened at the closing ceremony of the Games when the music track of the film was played even as about 3000 volunteers acted out the film. I cried that night too!

This film also won a gold at Cannes. So, what's better? Travelling in an Indian train or training from the Black Book of advertising? Don't get me wrong. I admire today's technology and its ability to give you unthinkable information and learning. However, if you want to add on to your Facebook learning, my suggestion is that you might be better off with face-to-face learning.

2
KINDERGARTEN TRUTHS ABOUT ADVERTISING

5

Don't Forget the Child in You

Cadbury was one of the first accounts that I worked on, but the brand wasn't Cadbury Dairy Milk. I was working on Bournvita, which wasn't the most exciting of brands, and in those days, certainly not one that was invigorating creatively. Most of the work was tactical, involving schemes ('get a mug free') and events (athletic contest, quiz contest).

Yet, I loved going to the Cadbury office. Cadbury occupied an entire colonial building on Peddar Road. One entered the building, stunned by well-maintained and polished wooden furniture, and by the carpets and the paintings on the wall. The products were all products everyone was familiar with and the company was one with a great reputation. In fact, in my earlier days, I had applied for the post of management trainee at Cadbury, only to be rejected.

The Cadbury business, especially Bournvita, was very important to Ogilvy. The account had been with Ogilvy since 1948; even now, Bournvita is our oldest continuing account.

In 1993, I was promoted to head creative at the Bombay office, and had not yet worked on the Cadbury Dairy Milk account. A series of events and circumstances however would ensure that I would handle the Cadbury account much sooner than any one of us in Ogilvy thought.

The brief from Cadbury: Get adults to eat chocolates.

In 1993, my brother Prasoon, his wife and I had gone on a holiday to the US to spend Diwali with my sister who lived in Michigan. While there, we used the Michigan house as our base as we did the usual things tourists are supposed to do. The first trip was to Disney World in Orlando. We packed light and off we went. We had a fantastic time in Disneyland, experiencing all the rides that we could afford.

From Orlando, we went to San Francisco, where we met my sister-in-law's uncle. He was seventy years old, and had recently undergone an angioplasty. He asked us whether we had tried a particular ride. When we said that we had, he said that he, too, had tried it and loved it when he had been to Disney a couple of months earlier. Some bells rang in my brain. A couple of months earlier? That would have been immediately after he had his stents put in—and I remembered that the ride was not recommended for anyone with a heart condition. When I asked him why he had tried the ride, he chuckled, saying that he wanted to check if the doctors had done their job well, and whether his heart would be able to take the excitement of the ride after the angioplasty.

The next day, we went to a toy store to pick up presents for Prasoon's son. We walked into a huge store, crowded with toys and customers. As we looked around, I saw a toy car emerge from under a table. Seconds later, a couple, both at least eighty years old, crawled out from under the table, chasing the toy car on all fours, laughing unabashedly. That image was instantly imprinted in my mind.

From San Francisco, we went to Hawaii. As soon as we checked into the hotel, I received a message that I should contact my sister urgently. When I did, she told me that Ranjan Kapur, my managing director, had called and wanted me to return to India immediately. I called Ranjan, only to learn that Cadbury was very unhappy with our work on Dairy Milk and had decided to put the account up for pitch. I didn't even have the time to pick up my luggage from Michigan (all I had in Hawaii were shorts and T-shirts).

My sister bought me a fresh ticket and I got on the flight, ruminating on the brief that Ranjan had given me. What was the brief? Simple. Cadbury wanted adults to eat chocolates. As I kept thinking about the brief, the only images I could see were of a seventy-year-old man with a heart condition on a dangerous ride and an eighty-year-old couple crawling on all fours behind a battery-operated car.

Don't let the child in you die. He or she is the genius. You are not.

Those images refused to go away. By the time the flight landed in Bombay, I had the campaign clearly thought through, and a song written at the back of my boarding card.

The lesson I learnt was that nobody rejuvenates the child in you like Disney does. They come up with human stories that touch parents and children alike. They have the purity of a child's thinking, and messages which are woven without preaching.

My brother Prasoon and I were lucky that Lalit Modi (who then had the franchise for Disney in India) asked us to adapt *Aladdin* and *The Lion King* in Hindi. I think we were reborn when we worked on these projects. The waiter in the hotel where we were working must have thought that these two grown-ups had gone mad—all we did was watch animation films, laughing, crying, taking notes and drinking beer. We were practically reliving our childhood and adapting it for India.

What did I learn from the Cadbury experience? Or from Disney for that matter? Don't let the child in you die. He or she is the genius. You are not.

6

The Human Behind the Client

Our preconceived notions make us label people and slot them into boxes. Much as we try not to do so, we do, and often lose out on opportunities and relationships.

Often, we write off people as 'the MBA', 'that brand manager', 'that marketing manager', and we forget that there is a human being behind the designation or the business card. We all need to look for the human being behind the manager, behind the designation.

I often work with big companies. The larger the client, the more likely that the company will have systems, processes and rules, all of which can irritate us. We say that the client is too process driven, that he uses research as a crutch, and so on. Over the years, I've learnt to be patient with the systems and the processes, much as juniors in large advertising agencies learn to deal with the systems and processes that we have. The more patient I get, the more I am able to respect the individual behind the client. Once one accepts the realities of the processes, one instantly becomes part of a team. For example, the client may tell you that he *has* to put the idea to test before clearing a script. If this is viewed as a challenge for the entire team, the understanding that each has for the other's problems deepens and empathy increases. Finally, you reach a stage when the process is a blur, a necessary chore.

Then you become friends with the client.

In perception, there can be no client with more systems and processes than Hindustan Unilever. Worse, it's packed with MBAs, managers, brand managers, brand directors, directors, marketing heads, and so on. And yet, it's with clients at Hindustan Unilever that I've seen rules being bent, broken and destroyed.

There are two great stories that I will always remember about Unilever managers. The first was when my father passed away suddenly, in Jaipur in February 1985. I was in Delhi, on a market visit for Unilever. As soon as I received the news, the Unilever colleagues accompanying me organized a car and a driver to take me to Jaipur. Halfway to Jaipur, the driver stopped at a restaurant, stating that he had been instructed to ensure that I ate something on the way. The driver was insistent even though I was in no mood to eat. He succeeded. When we reached my house in Jaipur, I was greeted outside the house by a gentleman dressed in a safari suit. He told me that he was from Hindustan Lever and handed over an envelope containing Rs 10,000. He said that, under the circumstances, I might not have the time to arrange cash from the bank. I didn't take the money, but the generosity of the gesture stayed with me forever.

The second incident happened in December 1983, when my good friend Arun Lal was getting married in Calcutta. Arun is so close to me that I obviously wanted to attend the wedding, but my workload—in my first year at Ogilvy—was a problem. Sunlight Detergent powder was launching in Calcutta—for the eastern zone—in January, so things were pretty hectic. Despite the situation, I walked up to my boss and asked her for a week off. Expectedly, she asked me how I could think of taking a week off for a friend's wedding when there was so much happening. She added however that she was fine with it if the client was—believing that the client would never be okay with it. So, I met Ravi Dhariwal, who was the brand manager, and explained the situation. In a matter of minutes, he solved the problem. He asked me to go ahead for the wedding, with a commitment from me that I would spend a couple of hours each day keeping tabs on the launch. He spoke to my boss and squared it with her.

What rules? What processes? Ravi Dhariwal, brand manager, Unilever, displayed heart here. It's been thirty-two years since Ravi helped me out to attend a wedding. In March 2015, I went to attend Ravi's son's wedding in Delhi, where this motley crew of old Unilever hands and those who worked with them shared this great story of Arun Lal's wedding. It's been years since Ravi and I have done business, but the relationship has become stronger with each passing year.

So you see, we must try to find and understand the human being behind the client. Once we see each other as human beings, it becomes the start of an enduring relationship. It allows us to understand limitations, positions and points of view, and prevents us from passing uninformed judgements.

It's when you see your clients as human beings that you discover many fine people. Over the years, I have learnt that there are companies like Unilever, Cadbury and Asian Paints that have the knack of hiring wonderful human beings—and this cannot be a coincidence. It has to be a system—the very system we are so quick to dismiss with contempt.

It is then no coincidence that some of my 'clients' are wonderful human beings—and many are no longer my clients, but my dear friends. All of us have to navigate the systems in our companies, but by acknowledging it, I have had the opportunity to work with, know and become friends with Muktesh Pant, Sanjay Khosla, Vindi Banga, Harish Manwani and many, many others over the years.

Staying on the subject of preconceived notions, let me move from the 'MBA' to the 'boring, non-creative' client. If the 'MBA' is a pain, the client who does not allow creativity is the most feared and the most hated—and a punishment posting as far as a creative professional is concerned.

When I was put on to the Pidilite account, I approached it with great trepidation. I was told the category was boring, the client didn't allow for creativity, and the budgets were small and insignificant. When I started working on the account, I discovered that all that Pidilite wanted was great creativity that worked for the brand; there were no other limitations. There was no interference once an idea had been agreed to, there were no painful meetings and no research. When I look back at my entire career, there has been no company that has won me more recognition, awards, accolades and respect than Pidilite. Over the decades, beginning with the late Mr B.K. Parekh and continuing to the current Madhukar Parekh, I've discovered that this 'lala' company has developed great judgement of what works and what does not; it has more respect for the creator than many 'professional' companies, and backs good ideas with all the resources that they deserve. And, together, we create work that wins for its brands. Incidentally, we have also become good friends. I look back and I wonder, what if I had wriggled out of the Pidilite account based on my preconceived notions?

Don't be scared of systems and processes. There are ways to fool them. I found at least a hundred. You will find more.

Or imagine this. I'm on holiday in Hawaii—the first time in my life that I've been abroad. My boss asks me to cut my holiday short, as a client, Cadbury, has threatened to sack us. I return and make my presentation to the client, the very man who destroyed my holiday. The moment we end the presentation, the client, Rajeev Bakshi, walks up to me, hugs me, and tells us that the account remains with Ogilvy. What if I saw Rajeev as an unhappy and ignorant client, rather than as a client who had a business challenge that we had to solve? Then, we wouldn't have retained the Cadbury account, and Rajeev wouldn't have become one of my closest friends.

Stay focused on the challenges of the brief and the client, and you become closer. This happens when you stop working at cross purposes and see a common enemy. To do that, get rid of all the preconceived notions and understand the systems, processes and rules that you must navigate and manage—all of it together.

Don't be scared of systems and processes. There are ways to fool them. I found at least a hundred. You will find more.

7

Scratching beneath the Surface

I have dismissed research time and again, privately and in public forums. It's time to clarify. I reject the procedures that I have seen, but I don't undervalue homework and thoroughness. And let me tell you I have attended more research sessions than most creative people.

So, what are the kinds of research I don't agree with? I hate researches where regular human beings are asked stupid questions. Obviously, you will get a stupid reply. You must imagine a situation when you show a pack of a new product to a housewife and ask, 'What do you feel on seeing this pack?' She feels bloody nothing. But she is in a group of people and she concocts something to save her face. The next respondent in the room has it easy. She says, 'I feel the same.' And so the chain goes on. Soon, a conclusion is forwarded as God's own truth. I have heard these housewives whisper after the group session, 'Did you understand the stupid questions they asked us?' I have also heard the reply, 'Doesn't matter, we got a free tiffin carrier and snacks, let's go home.'

Then there were other stupid techniques. They took me for some research, many decades ago, and put me behind a one-way mirror and gave me headphones. I threw the headphones away. The client complained, 'Why are you not using the headphones?

You won't hear the respondents.' I distinctly remember telling him, 'I don't want to hear stupid answers to stupid questions. I would much rather watch their body language. If they are chatting and not looking at the TV commercial after five seconds, we have lost them. If the body language is attentive, engaged and involved, we have got them. Simple!

Then came one funny meter, a machine out of *Star Wars*. The respondents were to hold the damn thing and rotate a dial to indicate when they lost interest and when they were really excited. All this for a thirty-second commercial. The ladies used it the same way a steering wheel is used by a child in a parked car. Swing it around, it's great fun; nobody will die. But a good idea won't be born, either. Now I believe there are researches studying the brain to know its response to advertising. Take it easy, folks.

Most of my work would not have seen the light of day if it had gone through this kind of research. The Cadbury Dairy Milk girl dancing on the cricket field would have become a saint if she had been pre-tested. Most of the Fevicol work would not have happened because 'we did not show furniture'. The Zoozoos of Vodafone would be aliens on earth. And Piyush Pandey would be a failed cricketer selling potatoes because he couldn't pass the 'link' test of advertising.

I am happy doing homework and chatting with people, without any agenda. I have often tried to articulate my distrust and lack of confidence in research and, perhaps, I have impatiently dismissed the concept.

I hate researches where regular human beings are asked stupid questions. Obviously, you will get a stupid reply.

As I sit down to write this book, I have the luxury of time and the number of words to clearly describe why I have reservations on research as we know it. To me, 'knowing' what consumers want after conducting some research is like saying 'I know Goa' after spending a week there on a conducted tour. All I would know is what the guide chose to show me—and there's certainly a lot more to Goa than that, much more. It's like the tip of the iceberg that research shows us, when the larger mass of the berg is invisible to us.

Research captures what's on the surface. It does not capture what's inside. It doesn't truly capture what drives consumers, what motivates them, what captures their imagination, what they want to hear, and so on.

Most of you have been to Goa and believe that you know Goa well. We're sitting in my house in Goa as we write this book, but believe me, it's not the Goa you know. We're in a small village called Guirim in the district of Bardez. There is no beach anywhere around, there is no shack, there are no bikini-clad women in sight. This is a village surrounded by paddy fields. A village without a single shop. We have snakes slithering around the fields, sometimes entering our garden. Our dogs (six of them) cannot be let out into the garden or the fields unless accompanied by someone keeping a careful lookout for snakes.

Everything around the house is green.

The village is sleepy; hardly any cars come here. We have a few regular visitors, all welcome ones. Each day, fresh bread is delivered by a baker on a cycle, tooting his horn as he reaches each house. Around 11 a.m., fish is delivered by the local fisherman. He, too, is on a cycle, tooting a different horn. A not-so-regular visitor is the chap who delivers gas cylinders.

By now, I think you get the picture. You have a fair idea of what Guirim is like and what these villagers might buy.

So you think. In addition to the breadwallah and the fisherman, we have a third daily visitor. This guy sells Walls ice cream. Would research have thrown that up? If you have transport, you can get anything that you want after a fifteen-minute drive, but what are the items my fellow villagers want delivered? Bread, fish and ice cream!

As I spend more time in this non-tourist side of Goa, I discover a completely different Goa from the one that we see when we come for weekend breaks or for off-sites and conferences. I've seen many species of birds, including kingfishers, hornbills and woodpeckers. Kingfishers? But where's the fish, I wonder. As I watch the kingfishers, I realize that they've adapted to the environment, diving into the paddy fields to catch worms and other small creatures. Do you know this Goa? If you want to understand, appreciate and love this Goa, get away from the beach. Explore the non-beach, non-shack, non-casino Goa. Then you will discover freshly baked poi and the fresh catch of fish that comes to your kitchen.

Miles Young, the Global CEO of Ogilvy, insists on eating local food wherever he goes. The last time he was in Delhi (for a board meeting), he dragged all of us to Chandni Chowk (where he goes during most visits to Delhi) for a meal. Some time back, Miles was in Bangalore for a large internal meeting on digital. The colleague who had ordered the lunch had arranged a north Indian menu, and Miles would have nothing of it. 'In south India, I want south Indian food,' said Miles, and that was the end of that.

Miles takes this experimentation and immersion to an extreme—that's his form of research. As far as possible, Miles wants to avoid the predictable five-star fare. It allows him to see, up close, how people live when he experiences what and how they eat. That's research.

Research of the real kind destroys presumptions and teaches us things that the tourist or superficial research never can. For example, I remember shooting at a little hill station in Gujarat called Saputara. To begin with, I hadn't known previously that there was a hill station in Gujarat. Saputara is on the border of Maharashtra and Gujarat. We were with Mr Amitabh Bachchan to shoot a story on the tribals of the region for Gujarat Tourism. We were talking about the tribal cuisine and their pickle made out of bamboo. As per the script, Mr Bachchan was to do a shot with the locals, eating their food. The wonderful tribal hosts served him (and all of us working on the shoot) a chapatti-like bread—almost red in colour, cooked in earthenware over a slow fire—and bamboo pickle. I didn't know that you could make pickle out of bamboo. After tasting this fare, all of us decided that we would continue eating the local food and not the stuff from the city that we had brought with us.

That's research. Understanding what people eat, where they live, how they live, what pleases them, displeases them . . . that's research. This is going beyond the tip of the iceberg; it's like going underwater and marvelling at the berg that we don't get to see.

*

What you see today of Cadbury's entry into the traditional sweetmeat market is the result of a process that began in the 1980s. Meena Kaushik and I used to travel to small towns and cities to see how (and what) sweets were served and consumed in homes there. We used to travel to small places, and small cities like Varanasi, Patna and Kanpur, across the country. We would try to understand the role of chocolates, to see whether chocolates had replaced the traditional mithai in any house; if so, we wanted to know why the shift happened.

Similarly, when Ogilvy was working on the National Literacy Mission, Roda Mehta and I travelled across the country trying to understand the problem better, what it would take to address the issue, what would motivate people to want to be literate, and so on. While on this study, we went to a place called Barabanki, which is a couple of hours from Lucknow. On the drive back to Lucknow, we stopped at a roadside stall to have tea. We watched, fascinated, as someone was deep-frying water chestnuts (*singhadas*, as we call them) and then coating them with salt and black pepper powder.

My curiosity piqued, I had to try it. I did; it was so magnificent that I asked Roda to try it as well. Roda, for those who do not know her, is the archetypal Parsi. Immaculately dressed and groomed—and extremely hygiene conscious. The moment I offered the fried singhadas to her, I regretted it, expecting her to ask whether the oil was safe or adulterated or recycled, and so on. To my surprise, Roda didn't do any of these things; she took one, then another and another, eating them with great joy.

Working on the National Literacy Mission campaign was rich research for me.

For Roda, I think it was the joy of discovering something new that caused her to break from her routine and imbibe the spirit of adventure, of experiencing the unknown.

Many young creative professionals in India think of research as a nuisance—probably influenced by me. It was not that I was born hating research; in my earlier days, I attended several meetings with researchers and numerous focus-group interviews. Most of the research studies threw up 'insights' that I had known since I was three years old—so this kind of 'research' became a waste of time for me.

The premium paid for authenticity was worth every rupee.

I still enjoy researching in smaller towns, small houses, and meeting people. Staying in these places for a few days teaches you so much. You can see the food being cooked; you marvel at how six people live in a house of 300–400 square feet; you can experience the role of TV in their lives; you learn what one generation aspires to and what the next aspires to.

More than anything, this form of non-armchair research leaves you with thousands of images imprinted in your mind. How can I visualize something that I have never seen? How can I visualize a bamboo pickle or a small house in which six people live? How will I know the colours and the sounds that I need to recreate?

The simple answer is that I will have answers to none of these questions without research. Real research, that is, where you pack your bags, get out of your comfort zone and stop by the roadside to eat deep-fried singhadas.

This kind of research also tells you what you can recreate and what you cannot. For example, when we were shooting the bus film for Fevicol, we had two options. The first was to 'recreate' Rajasthan in Panvel and the second was to shoot on location in Rajasthan. The second option was Rs 12 lakh or so, more expensive. Madhukar Parekh asked me what Prasoon would prefer. I said he would prefer Rajasthan, but if there was a cost constraint, we could do it in Panvel.

We shot in Rajasthan. Every second of the film is authentic, and the authenticity shows. The film has run for ten years and could go on for another ten.

How could I have visualized Rajasthan if I hadn't 'researched' Rajasthan?

8

The Magic of Music

Music plays a huge role in any form of communication; after all, music is the very soul of our culture. As I write this, sitting in my house in Goa, it is a fortnight to the Ganapati festival. In about an hour, we will be surrounded by music, as makeshift choirs rehearse for their performances during the Ganapati celebrations.

So it is with every religious festival and every cultural festival in our country. Music is the core of the festival, connecting one and all at a purely emotional level. Many know the song (both the lyrics and the tune), some know just the tune and hum along, but even those who are listening to a song for the first time get involved. Music is a great connector, connecting even to those who are tone-deaf!

One would think that there is a lot of music in Indian advertising. But listen to a clutter tape of commercials and you will change your mind. There are a lot of jingles, but not much music. On the other hand, in Ogilvy's communication, there's a lot of music. Real music. And very few jingles.

The credit for this goes to Suresh Mullick. In the early eighties, jingles dominated the Indian advertising scene. It was about taking a brand name, slapping it on a tune, and repeating it a number of times. That was it. Remember 'Nirma, Nirma, Nirma, Nirma, washing powder Nirma', and so on.

That wasn't music—and that isn't music. Not to us at least.

Suresh Mullick, who was my boss and the national creative director, had a fantastic sense of and appreciation for music. He hated the thought of a song 'selling' a product, but wanted the music and the song to entertain, touch and involve the listener. He had to fight the trend of the stereotypical jingle, and he succeeded when he created 'Sometimes Cadbury can say it better than words', with singer Usha Uthup. That was in 1982.

And Mullick's reputation (and Ogilvy's) as someone who understood music received a huge fillip in 1986 when he created '*Mile sur mera tumhara*'.

By this time, Suresh was clear that music would play a role in every good piece of communication. Not a jingle, but a song and music. Around this time, I was working on a campaign for the National Literacy Mission (NLM), which had music by the renowned composer and singer Suresh Wadkar. When Mullick heard the piece, he was disappointed, saying that I was forcing the music and the song on to the consumer, that the work was too literal. He suggested that I try classical music, and play a raag.

I remembered a song we had created for a Unilever launch of Sunlight Detergent Powder; it was called '*Purab se surya uga*', which would fit the NLM perfectly. I requested Unilever for permission to use the song, and, thankfully, they agreed because it had been used only for their internal audience at a conference.

Suresh Mullick taught me (and Ogilvy) many lessons. The first is not to create music and lyrics that take the brief literally. The second is never to force music onto the consumer. The third is not to 'sing' brand names.

We stopped singing brand names. And each time someone pushes us into it, we push back, agreeing only to use it in the voice-over. Till today, by and large, thanks to Suresh Mullick, we stick to these simple rules in our TVCs (television commercials).

In many ways, Suresh was thinking like David Ogilvy. David used to say that an ad should not come and shout out at the consumer, saying, 'Hello, I am an ad. Can you be part of my life?' He wanted us to make ads less literal, much as Suresh wanted the music not to sound or feel like music created for an ad.

Suresh Mullick's diktat: Never sing brand names.

We took a lot of pride in making our music less literal, and each time we slipped or were pressured into doing so, it bothered me, as it did when, in the early nineties, we created '*Tan ki shakti, mann ki shakti*' for Bournvita. In the version we presented, there was no 'Bournvita' in the song. We tried arguing, saying that it was obvious that Bournvita was the 'singer' and that there was no need to mention the name. The client insisted and, finally, under pressure, we sort of stuck the brand name at the end of a line.

Thankfully, over the years, clients have evolved, and are less and less insistent on this issue.

Don't get me wrong. There are opportunities to name the brand multiple times, and yet entertain and engage the viewer. We've done it a number of times—most beautifully for Close-Up, when we created '*Close-Up kyu nahi karte hai*'. Since the name of the toothpaste allowed us to pun with the word 'close-up', the lyrics described someone with fresh breath being able to get close up to someone from the opposite gender; and this was done in a manner that entertained the viewer though the brand name was mentioned multiple times.

The punning possibilities with Close-Up allowed us to break Suresh's rule.

'You have created the most original piece of work. Now write an original song,' I said.

Similarly, in a Madhya Pradesh Tourism ad, we have a salesman extolling the virtues of MP, singing, '*MP ajab hai*'. Each time he shows you a new tourism landmark, he repeats the name of the state. Again, the use of 'MP' doesn't irritate, because it is seen as the natural behaviour of a salesman. If you look at the tone of the salesman who is singing it, it is almost like a tourist guide singing things to you. So, there is a suspension of disbelief and you are entertained, almost forgetting that there is a brand pitching it to you.

Even great scripts get lifted by great music. After Mahesh and Rajiv had shot the very first Vodafone pug film, they layered some stock music and showed the film to me. The film was fantastic, and I was most concerned about the music. When I asked them what they had planned for the music, Mahesh told me that they would buy the rights to an existing song. I was aghast. 'You have created the most original piece of work. Now write an original song,' I said. 'I am not a lyricist,' was Mahesh's reply. 'You don't have to be a lyricist. Mahesh, this is a "feel" film. Write what you feel about this film. I want you to give it a shot tonight. I want you to meet me tomorrow morning and share your thoughts,' I said.

That night Mahesh wrote, 'You and I in this beautiful world'.

The rest is history. The music is legendary, as is the song. It's hummed, people sing along with the music when they hear it, and many still have the song as their ringtone!

Now just imagine the same film with a lifeless track. That is what music does to a film.

While I believed that the pug film required original music, there are times when someone has already written a song or a piece of music that fits your script perfectly.

My memory bank is filled with songs that I've heard; songs in Hindi, Rajasthani, or in dialects from Uttar Pradesh. My knowledge of English songs is restricted to the songs one hears at friends' houses. Popular songs like 'Come September'. My wife, Nita, however, is just the opposite; she was brought up surrounded by English songs, to the extent that her mother used songs as devices to teach her various things. For example, Nita told me about a song called 'Little Boxes' that her mother would sing to her to help her remember colour names. It's a song made famous by Pete Seeger, and it's absolutely delightful. The song is

Every memory is an opportunity. One of Nita's favourite songs inspired this TVC.

a political satire about suburban development and the resultant conformist middle-class attitudes, where all the houses looked the same and had similar ambitions and aspirations. 'Little boxes on the hillside, little boxes made of ticky-tacky, little boxes, little boxes, little boxes, all the same. There's a green one and a pink one. And a blue one . . .'

We were working on a commercial for Maruti where we wanted to refer to all other cars as being boxy, as being the same. That's when I remembered Nita and 'Little Boxes'. We listened to the song again and again, and then shared it with Mayank Pareek, then head of marketing, Maruti. He bought the idea in exactly five minutes and we were able to create a wonderful commercial with pure and pristine music. The music in an ad film should not intrude or intimidate. It must live the script and entertain, involve and engage the viewer. If the Vodafone music was completely original and the Maruti film was not, the signature tune that Suresh Mullick used for Titan was a perfect example of inspiration. Suresh used a Mozart tune as the signature, getting musicians to interpret the tune in their own fashion to reflect the script. And as the original piece was more than two hundred years old, there was no copyright issue to deal with.

The music in an ad film should not intrude or intimidate. It must live the script and entertain, involve and engage the viewer.

It was in 1987 that the first Titan film was made with this music. Last year, in 2014, after twenty-seven years we did a film based on a medical school with the same music. Consumers have changed, the product has changed, the country has changed, but the music has endured.

When creative directors put their heart and soul into the music, they build an asset that can be used, as has been the case with Titan, for decades.

The Titan tune is now an asset that has lasted decades.

Take Lifebuoy's '*Raksha karta hai Lifebuoy*'. If you listen to the words, which include the brand name, it sounds like a sales pitch. But that's not how consumers hear the song; they immerse themselves in the music, they hum along with the music.

These are just a few instances of what music can do for a script or a brand. That's why it gets on my nerves when a client says, 'Buy some stock music and slap it on,' or 'Can't we get the music cheaper?'

What is the return that Titan has got out of their investment in the Mozart tune, or Unilever got out of the investment in Lifebuoy? How much is it worth to Vodafone each time someone hums, 'You and I'?

We are a country where there is magical music from all regions. Listen to it. Respect it. Get inspired by it. Inspire others with it.

9

The Flea in the Tail of a Racehorse

India has a supreme fascination for movie stars and cricketers, with the result that almost every third commercial that we see features one of the two categories.

What astonishes me is that so many of the commercials that feature these celebrities (especially cricketers) are terrible. The reason for this is that agencies and clients and creative people get lazy the moment they have a star—they think the job is done.

What I've learnt about working with movie stars and cricketers is the opposite. Once you have a famous personality, you need to work ten times harder on every single aspect of the communication. For example, when you work on a script that features a cricketer, you need to remember that most cricketers are not good actors (just as most actors would fail if cast as cricketers) and will not be able to effectively deliver 'lines'. It's easy to write a script for a film star because he or she is an actor. Many TVCs featuring film personalities are well received despite the scripts being weak or poor. I've always believed that if you don't work hard on these scripts, your contribution is akin to the flea in the tail of a racehorse that wins, and the flea believes that it has won the race.

When you work with a celebrity, the viewer must find the celebrity, the script and the idea memorable, not just the celebrity.

For many celebrities, acting in a campaign is a transaction. They come to the sets for a defined period of time, perform and go. For them to think of their role as more than just a transaction, you need to work on the script and get them excited about it.

That's why I work so hard on any campaign that features celebrities—and I've worked with a lot of them.

Of all the celebrities, I have had no greater joy (and pressure) than working with Amitabh Bachchan. His dedication to the craft and to the job is admirable.

When you work with a celebrity, the viewer must find the celebrity, the script and the idea memorable, not just the celebrity.

Mr Bachchan discusses the script in great detail before a shoot; he discusses the background, the context, the impact that the ad is expected to make. I've shot with him and lived with him for days together shooting various campaigns in Gujarat. I've shot with him in between shoots (for his films for other brands, whenever he could find the time) for the polio-eradication campaign. I have shot at leisure and shot with him in time constraints and limitations. He is so involved and conscious of the fact that he has to deliver, that almost every Amitabh Bachchan commercial is well received, even if the script is weak. He will stay up at night before a morning shoot discussing a script. He makes his suggestions, and, if I say, 'No, Mr Bachchan, I think my idea is better . . .' he will say, 'Let me think about it.' He has no qualms about saying, 'You were right, I was wrong.' All he cares about is a good film at the end of all our efforts.

The greatest example of commitment and sense of responsibility: Mr Bachchan.

Working with Mr Bachchan teaches you about your own profession or craft, and also teaches you about life, culture, literature, music and customs. He also teaches you about work ethic and commitment to your tasks. I was with him in Gujarat, in the middle of the Gir forest, when he called me to his room and made me listen to a recitation of his father, Harivanshrai Bachchan's '*Madhushala*'. He was reciting it in preparation for a recitation that he would do in Paris in the next few weeks. Though he had heard his father's recitation many, many times, he wanted it to be perfect. This is the level of his commitment.

When I approached him for the Cadbury communication so as to address the infestation problem, he wanted to know all the details as the issue had captured the attention of the media and the consumer at large. Bharat Puri made a PowerPoint presentation to Mr Bachchan to explain the problem, as well as Cadbury's proposed response and other relevant details. Mr Bachchan asked question after question, saying that the product was consumed by children, so he needed to be absolutely certain that what he would say in the communication was, indeed, the truth. This wasn't about commerce; he needed to be absolutely convinced that he was doing the right thing. Once he was convinced, as he later said, he didn't need to 'perform'. He had internalized the issue and his performance mirrored his conviction.

There are many other things that one can learn from Mr Bachchan. In general, he is never late. On the odd occasion when he believes that he will be late, he will inform you in advance. Recently, he drove in from Nashik for a shoot, and the traffic held him up. He reached the studio late, at about 9.30 p.m. We had originally planned to shoot from 8 p.m. to midnight, so I suggested that we finish two out of the four planned films that night and reschedule the other two for a future date. He refused, suggesting that we get on with it and finish all four that night.

On another shoot, one of the first shots planned was a scene where he is reading from 'Madhushala'. The copy that we had sourced him was in a small format. Mr Bachchan said he would get a larger copy from his house and that we could do that particular scene later. This, from a man who had driven from Nashik, and was faced with the prospect of shooting all night. Anyone else would have shot with the smaller edition and just got on with it, but Mr Bachchan, like many great people, believes that God is in the details.

Besides being extremely hard-working and thorough, Mr Bachchan is also a perfectionist. After finishing a shot, he looked at me and said, 'So, Piyush?' and I replied, 'Fantastic take, sir.' He said, 'No, I will do one more.' This has happened so many times that I cannot count. He will decide that he is not satisfied with his performance and insist on a retake, even if it is late and even if he is tired. That's the huge lesson for all of us; imagine any of us asking a colleague or a junior for feedback on work. To be able to do what Mr Bachchan does so effortlessly is to be naturally magnanimous and humble.

Barring the vices which he doesn't have and I do, Mr Bachchan and I share a work ethic: commitment to work, the team, and the brand we're working on. The reason that I get along so well with Mr Bachchan is that, like him, I am an early riser irrespective of what time I go to sleep. In addition, I hate being late for any meeting with anyone.

Newcomers at Ogilvy had to learn this the hard way. When the fresh recruits first partied with me, they would be gently warned about the next morning—that I would not tolerate anyone coming late to the office. We could have been out drinking till 3 a.m., but I would reach the office at Kamala Mills by 9.15 a.m. The official 'office time' to be at work is 9.30 a.m. At 9.35 a.m., I would place Post-it notes on the desks of those who hadn't come in yet, saying, 'I'm missing you.' By 9.55 a.m., another Post-it would be added, saying, 'God! I am really missing you, it is 10 o'clock.' The message went home. It took no shouting and no memos to create a culture where everyone was on time and punctual for all the meetings.

Punctuality is one of the most important virtues of advertising. If you cause a delay in the start of a meeting between the client and the agency, you could often be costing both tens of thousands of rupees, sometimes lakhs of rupees. If you delay a shoot, it could be many times more, and such costs are irresponsible and unacceptable.

Nowadays, I do not attend many shoots, but in the days that I did attend, I would make it a point to be on the sets well before I was required to be there. As a result, many production houses tell me that it is an absolute pleasure working with Ogilvy. And I think, if Amitabh Bachchan can be disciplined, involved, responsible and cost-conscious, how can we not?

In the early days of my career, I would wake up early in the morning and buy copies of all the newspapers when a new campaign would break. I feel my job is not over till I am satisfied that the ad has been reproduced well, and that we have received feedback on it.

Accepting feedback, good or bad, is crucial in advertising where the audience is the ultimate judge. More importantly, we need to rid ourselves of professional insecurities. The moment we can ask virtually anyone working with us for feedback, we increase the opportunities of improving the film with their inputs.

Mr Bachchan has underlined, in many conversations with me, that he is always nervous before a shoot. Not sometimes, but always. He tells me the day you stop getting nervous, the day you think you have arrived, is when the downfall begins.

Ever since he first shared this with me, I'm consciously nervous before and during a campaign. Those who work with me will agree. If I could rephrase Mr Bachchan: *to stay relevant, stay nervous. Very nervous.*

Another star I admire is Aamir Khan.

Aamir's cousin, Mansoor Khan, who directed *Qayamat se Qayamat Tak*, is a friend of mine. I remember I was invited to a preview of the film in 1998, which is when I first met Aamir. Little did I realize that Aamir would be the thinking man's actor of the next generation—or that I would work with him in future.

The first time that we worked together was for Titan, and so much of Aamir reminded me of Amitabh Bachchan. There was meticulousness in his approach, a need to know more, an involvement and patience, all hallmarks of Mr Bachchan. Aamir was in no great hurry with the pre-production meetings—he wanted to understand the brand, the script, the context, the business objective, and so on.

The first set of commercials that I did with Aamir was rooted in another relationship: the relationship between my major-domo, the late Ghoshto, and me. It was a relationship of great mutual respect, where Ghoshto, essentially my house help, could take great liberties with me and joke at my expense even in the presence of others, in the same manner that Aamir's butler does with him in the Titan film.

Aamir spent some time with the late Vihang Nayak who was an actor in the Marathi theatre circuit, chatting with him and getting to understand him better. Then Aamir, Prasoon (who was directing the films) and Vihang Nayak sat together to discuss the shoot.

What was apparent was that Aamir had the greatest respect for his fellow actor, so Vihang Nayak's role was discussed to extract the maximum out of his performance, not just Aamir's.

Meticulous in approach, a need to know more, involved and patient: Aamir Khan.

It was these discussions that caused magic to happen to the Titan–Ogilvy–Aamir–Vihang–Prasoon team. It is difficult to pinpoint how much Aamir contributed to the Titan journey, but the least I can say is that it was significant. All of us discussed each script, with Aamir adding touches and nuances that lifted the story and the performances, the nudges that make a thoroughly enjoyable script even more enjoyable. Aamir also contributed to locations and to the look of the set, all the while remembering that the client was Titan, the director was Prasoon, and I was part of the creative agency.

It's difficult to say whether Aamir or Mr Bachchan are celebrities or brand ambassadors when they come with us on a shoot, or are an extended part of my creative team. They're not driven by their egos; they become part of the creative process. A common goal emerges: a great piece of communication. Most importantly, no suggestion is selfishly motivated, so the consequent decisions are healthy and constructive, making the process more enriching and productive.

In most cases, celebrities do not add to a creative idea or to a script; they are constraints and handicaps. All they want to do is get off the set as soon as the contracted time is over, whether the film works for the client or not. They display little or no involvement with the idea, but treat the whole experience as something that's got to be done before they move on to other commitments.

Aamir, Mr Bachchan and a few others work hard on the campaigns they sign on. As a result, almost all their work is enjoyable (even work that is not done by us). Take Aamir and the commercial for Innova which isn't our film. The fact that Aamir is in multiple (seven) roles in the film gives one an idea of the complexity: multiple make-up changes, multiple costume changes, multiple angles, and so on. This role couldn't have been done by a model or an actor who wanted it over and done with quickly; it would have involved in-depth discussions, debates and even arguments, with everyone in the team focused on one target: communication that works on the brief.

Prasoon and I shot for Four Square cricket gear, where the script wanted Sanjay Manjrekar and three other cricketers to 'row' a boat in Kerala with bats. The shot was difficult because we needed all four cricketers to synchronize their rowing actions. They needed to be in perfect rhythm, which unfortunately they just couldn't get right. All we needed was two seconds of synchronization. The cricketers were getting tired and impatient. Just when it looked like we might have to compromise on the shoot, Sanjay Manjrekar called the other three cricketers and said to them, 'Listen, guys, this man [Prasoon] is trying his best to make us look great; we have to try harder for ourselves, we have to help him make us look great.'

This is what celebrities have to think about. The final product is as much a reflection of them as it is of us. In the case of really big-name celebrities, it's perhaps a greater reflection of them than of us.

Some brand ambassadors understand how hard agencies and directors work.

10

Select Your Sounding Boards

I've been blessed with a lot of sounding boards in my life. The greatest sounding boards have been in my family, with each of them being creative as well as having a point of view. For instance, I scribble down an idea for a TVC and I call up my sister to share it with her. She says, '*Haan*, nice.' Five minutes later, the phone rings and it's my sister sharing some constructive thoughts on the idea.

Within the family, the greatest sounding board is Prasoon, my brother. Since he is in the same profession as me, his feedback is far more detailed and precise. I read out a script to him and he would say something like, 'It is a fantastic script, but not good enough for Fevicol.' It takes Prasoon only a few seconds to say these few words, but for me, it's a precise judgement. The idea goes into the wastebasket and I go back to the drawing board. Then there are two people for me as good as family. One is Himmat Singh in Jaipur, a theatre and culture expert. The other is K.K. Raina, actor and director of theatre and movies. Both are experts and fearless friends of mine who can tell me, 'Sorry, this is a bad idea.'

There is a saying in Hindi, '*Nindak neere raakhiye*', which translates to 'Keep your critics near you'. This is because there is always an abundance of people who want to say good things to you, but a shortage of candid critics. If Prasoon had not been there to kill that Fevicol idea, I might have thought it good enough to present to the client—and he would have rejected it. The rejection by a well-wisher saves one's time. You know early on that an idea is weak or not good enough, which gives you more time to think through a stronger, better idea. The important thing is to look for those who have no axe to grind, who have only your interest in mind. Let me share a story about Ghoshto, my man Friday. Ghoshto was with me for years as a cook, caretaker, manager and friend. As he would be in and out of the rooms in the house, he used to hear all the discussions that took place. He was, in fact, privy to all ideas and films before our clients heard or saw them. And because he was opinionated, vocal and intelligent, he became a great sounding board for me.

It's important to get feedback from the consumer—even your house help.

There was an occasion when two big TVCs were released at the same time and I showed them to Ghoshto. The first was a beautifully shot and deeply emotional film for Nokia, and the second was an entertaining film for Cadbury Perk (the one where the bride is munching Perk under her wedding veil). Once he had seen both the films, Ghoshto passed his judgement: the Nokia film will win awards and the Perk film will sell loads of chocolate. And that's exactly what happened.

Before Sonal went to Malaysia, he was a great sounding board. Abhijit, Rajiv and my colleagues in creative are all sounding boards.

It's fantastic when I can walk up to a junior colleague and share an idea. I love it when I see his or her face changing, and he or she thinking that the idea is rubbish. I don't even need to hear their view; I know the idea is dead. But the upside of sounding boards is invaluable. There's a film that most of you would have seen, the 'M-Seal Will' TVC, which I touch upon later in the book.

I had completed writing the entire script, down to the last detail. The few friends and colleagues that I had bounced it off all thought that we had a complete winner. In the original script, in the idea that I had fleshed out in detail, the drop of water obliterated the signature on the will. I was making the drop fall on the signature. I called up Abhijit early the next morning and told him that I had a mother of an idea for M-Seal, and proceeded to read out the script. He was silent as he heard me, and silent for a few seconds after I finished, absorbing all that I'd said. Finally, he responded, 'Mama, this is a truly fantastic idea. However, I have one suggestion to make. In your idea, the drop of water falls on the signature. Instead, let the drop fall on the digit 1 that precedes the many zeroes, the drama is that much greater.'

Think of the drama: each zero that follows the one makes the sum of money larger, more powerful. Yet, however many zeroes there are, if the 1 does not exist, then the sum is reduced to nothing. Just bouncing the idea off Abhijit made a good idea great. That's the power of sharing ideas to get them validated—they could improve by leaps and bounds.

A good idea becomes great when you involve more minds.

The more insecure you are about your idea, the less you will share it and the less the possibility for a good idea to become great. Interestingly, I bounce ideas off seeming opponents—and have never lost out. Often, at a shoot with one director, I bounce off an idea that I propose to shoot with another. I've done this with so many directors, and have always found them generous and helpful. I was on a shoot with Shoojit Sircar and discussed an idea that I hadn't yet presented to the client. Shoojit shared his thoughts, which certainly helped me sharpen my thinking. Over the years, Rajiv Menon has been a great sounding board even if our paths cross less often and we hardly work with each other. Shoojit and Rajiv are great examples; I've bounced ideas off almost every film director that I've worked with, including Prasoon.

A lot of creative people don't share ideas, thanks to some fear that I'm not quite able to understand. What is it that we're working on? We're certainly not in the nuclear science business. Share the idea with as many people as you know and trust. Imagine, for a moment, that an idea you share is 'stolen' by the person you shared it with. But even in this situation, there is an upside. You learn that this particular person is not someone who can be trusted. Over a period of time, you will identify some people whose judgement you trust, whose opinions you value and respect, and whose suggestions you know will always be constructive and encouraging.

The more insecure you are about your idea, the less you will share it and the less the possibility for a good idea to become great.

It's no different from what we do with trust-related issues within our families. There are some people you find it easier to confide in, some whom you find it easier to trust, and others whom you do not. These lists get richer with experience, and finally, you know in milliseconds who would be the best sounding board in each situation.

The lovely part about sounding boards is that as the trust and experience between two people grow, so do the opportunities for each to be a sounding board, as Prasoon and I are to each other.

Take the silver at Cannes that Prasoon won for Enterprise Nexus for the Sony Ericsson 'One Black Coffee' film. One can talk about it now—that film was written by me. Prasoon had just done a film for Bajaj Sunny, which virtually put him on the map of directors. The now-famous Prasoon was approached by Rajiv Agarwal with a script for the mobile phone brand. Prasoon didn't like the script and told Rajiv so. Rajiv was fine with it, telling Prasoon, 'You come up with a great film, let it be your script.' So, Prasoon called me and shared the brief, asking me to write the script. It was New Year's Day, and Rajeev Bakshi was in Jaipur, spending the holiday with us in my family house. I cracked the idea, and that evening, Rajeev, Prasoon and I sat in Narayan Niwas, our self-appointed personal bar in Jaipur. As we brought in the New Year, we wrote the script and that was that. Later, Neil French learnt that I had written the script, and told the Ogilvy global creative council that if some of our own people were writing scripts for us, we would be winning silvers, and not other agencies.

11

Good Clients Get Good Work

The biggest rule of our business is that great clients get great work, good clients get good work and not-so-good clients get bad work. Great work is about partnerships—partnerships between an agency and a client. It is in this context that I call people great, good and not so good.

Unless you find the support, unless you find a believer, you can't do brave things. David Ogilvy once said, 'Don't keep a dog and bark yourself.' It's the same with clients who dictate advertising. As David said, it's like they have a dog and yet they are the ones who bark. If the client leaves us to do the barking, which is what they sign us on for in the first place, the relationship is richer—for both the client and for us.

It's not surprising then that the greatest work over the years has been for clients such as Pidilite, Asian Paints, Cadbury and Vodafone. They all understand and respect the roles in the partnership—and they all push us to be brave. Let me underline that these are not the only great clients—it's just that we have been able to work together for a greater length of time and have developed a greater body of memorable work. As far as I am concerned, 95 per cent of our clients have been great clients—and perhaps in some instances we have failed them and have been unable to give them the quality of work that they deserved.

When you think of the work as a partnership between an agency and a client, one quickly realizes that the agency cannot take credit for the great work done, for awards, for the praise in the media and other recognition. A great campaign needs the client to push, needs the client to repose confidence in you, for the client to allow you to flirt with the edges, for the client to motivate and encourage you.

We once did a campaign for the New Perk from Cadbury, and Bharat Puri was the client. At the time we were discussing the brief, India was consumed by its first much-publicized match-fixing scandal.

'*Hamam mein sab nange hain,*' (All are naked in the public bath) was a statement that was attributed to Kapil Dev in this context. Even though Kapil denied making such a statement, the attribution caused the phrase to go viral, though we were living in an era that was almost pre-Internet. To jog your memory, that was the time when Manoj Prabhakar and many others were being questioned about throwing away or fixing matches.

For New Perk, we recommended a take-off on this development. With the tagline '*Naye Perk ka Fark*', we created three commercials that immediately cued the match-fixing scandal, playing with 'who ate it up', which could mean either the money (which the match-fixers would have) or the chocolate (which was what we wanted to sell).

Bharat Puri cleared the campaign in a single, short meeting.

It was edgy stuff, almost a social commentary, something that brands were wary of doing at the time. We had pixelated the faces of the characters in the TVCs, and signed on Chetan Shashital, who is a genius when it comes to mimicking famous voices, to do the voice-overs. We created commercials that cued Ravi Shastri, Siddhu and Mohammad Azharuddin.

It was a challenging position for a brand to take. Would the angst over match-fixing be so deep that the consumers would not embrace the tongue-in-cheek humour of the communication? Would they laugh at the commercials or get upset with the more-than-obvious references to match-fixing, which was a very depressing and humiliating development for cricket fans? We believed that the Indian consumer was more than ready to laugh at the storylines and the innuendos—and Bharat Puri backed us to the hilt. The campaign was a big hit, and we, the client and Ogilvy, were delighted that we understood the new India.

The biggest rule of our business is that great clients get great work, good clients get good work and not-so-good clients get bad work.

Often, in business, risks need to be taken. But the risks are the risks an accomplished gambler takes, not the sucker who is born every minute. In the New Perk scenario, it was not as if we did not consider the possible downside. We did, and did everything that we believed would mitigate that risk, while keeping the excitement and freshness of the communication intact. For Bharat Puri, head of the India office of a global company, all decisions had to be made bearing in mind the impact any decision that he made could have on the global equity of his firm. For us at Ogilvy, we had to bear in mind that a faux pas in India on creatives for a global brand could have serious ramifications that went all the way up to WPP's head office.

It might have been easier to have come up with a 'safe' campaign. We chose not to and when the campaign caught the imagination of viewers across the country, we knew that the risk was a risk well taken.

Another brand, or rather company, that has taken great risks with us, is Pidilite. More recently, in 2014, you may recall the work for Fevicol during the election campaign (the three chairs) or for Fevikwik during the India–Pakistan World Cup match (the border). But these two examples are recent; the client's appetite for out-of-the box, clutter-cutting work has been decades old.

Pidilite has always been a big risk-taker.

Pidilite is now a huge company, with more than thirty-four brands. The bulk of the turnover comes from Fevicol, so it is not difficult to understand the client committing significant advertising and marketing spends to the brand. Fevikwik draws credibility directly from Fevicol, being in the same category (adhesive), but being a consumer product, enjoys better margins. Here, too, it is not difficult to understand Pidilite making investments in brand-building.

Madhukar Parekh, the chairman of Pidilite, briefed us on what was then a small brand, but a brand that he believed had great potential. The brand was M-Seal, an epoxy sealant. What did the product do? When we understood the applications and the simplicity of use, we, like Madhukar Parekh, thought we had a winner in our hands.

The final recommendation we made was a seventy-second commercial—at a time when we had not yet done a commercial of more than sixty seconds for the flagship brand Fevicol. The story was simple, but needed that duration to be told effectively. It didn't show the benefits of the application or use of the product; we showed the disadvantage of not having used the product! M-Seal could, among one of many applications, arrest leaks in ceilings and roofs. Our film showed a villainous protagonist getting his father, on his deathbed, to sign a will in his favour. Moments after the signature is on the will, a drop of water from a leaking ceiling causes the signature to get washed off. If only M-Seal had been used!

The communication worked wonders for the brand. Ten years after it was created, the ad is still played from time to time, without any editing or upgrade. The story is timeless.

It took a brave Madhukar Parekh to buy into the idea of the commercial—and allow us the duration that we believed would work best. In hindsight, the M-Seal commercial is truly a significant piece of work. It is easy to see that the genesis of a big work takes a big heart, big vision, big belief and big faith—in both the client and the agency.

Another brave client is Pranav Adani, our client for many years. In December 2014, he asked us to come and meet him in Ahmedabad as he had a challenge that he wanted to discuss. We met at the Taj, planning for a long evening. The conversation was about Fortune Cooking Oil, a brand that he believed needed rejuvenation. His brief was hardly a brief, or the perfect brief, depending on how one viewed it. '*Sabko rula de, yaar, aisa kuch bana ki voh ad na lage*,' he said, which translates to 'Create something that makes everyone cry, create something that doesn't look like an ad.'

That was the brief.

As the evening progressed, he added to the brief: '*Bahut samose tal liye, yaar, ab aisa kuch kar jo pahunche kahin*.' (Many samosas have been fried, create something that touches people.)

It's a brief that was, doubtless, challenging, but a brief that I loved. Pranav was telling me that he wanted a triple century—but not telling me how to make that triple century.

Big briefs like this are massive challenges—because the very freedom that you have been given puts pressure on you to come up with not just a good piece of work but a great piece of work. You keep writing down ideas and you keep rejecting them, as there is an element of the brief that the idea does not meet. In this case, the idea might meet the condition that there should be no depiction of frying, but might not tick the box that says the consumer should be so touched that he or she is fighting back tears.

It's high pressure. There is no pressure that is greater than great freedom and the consequent responsibility that comes with it. The greatest pressure came from the trust and faith that this Gujarati entrepreneur reposed in us. He expected nothing short of magic; anything less would be a let-down.

After many ideas were discussed and rejected, we finally had one that we truly believed would delight Pranav and meet all his requirements. There was no frying in the story; in fact, there wasn't a single shot of cooking or of the kitchen. The story brought tears to the eyes, and was, in our opinion, one that would be memorable and talked about. Finally, it was not just a century of an idea; it was a triple century of an idea.

The idea, in a nutshell, was this. A young man is in the hospital and yet to recover from his illness. His grandmother visits him in the hospital. She wants to feed him his favourite dal, which the nurse on duty refuses to allow, sticking to the rules that say that food cooked outside the hospital is not allowed. The disappointed grandmother, convinced that the grandson would improve once he had the dal, comes every day with her dal, attempting to convince the nurse to break the rules. Finally, she succeeds. When the young man is fed the dal, he shows immediate improvement, breaking into a hitherto-absent smile.

The film ends with a pack shot that shows Fortune Cooking Oil.

I called up Pranav and said that we were ready with the idea. 'I am ready. When can I come?' I asked. We met in Ahmedabad the next day, and I narrated the story to him. In a few minutes, it was clear that he, too, thought that the ad was exactly what he wanted, and gave us the go-ahead.

Angshu Malik, the marketing head, asked me what the length of the commercial would be. I couldn't answer, except to say that it would be 'longish' because we had to build up the tension between the three characters and we had to portray the grandmother's persuasion through different emotions. I asked him not to restrict the time, but to allow us the duration that would make the film a truly memorable one.

We knew that it would be a long film, but had little idea that, by the time we finished with the edit suite, it would be four minutes thirty-eight seconds long.

My colleague Sukesh and I roped in film director Vivek Kakkad, and began work on the script. We wrote and rewrote the dialogues (and the order of the dialogues) a number of times till we thought we had got it right. What should come first, the 'bribe', the 'cajoling', the 'tantrum'? We shuffled these till all of us were of the same view. As usual, I bounced the final script off a few close colleagues and friends for confirmation.

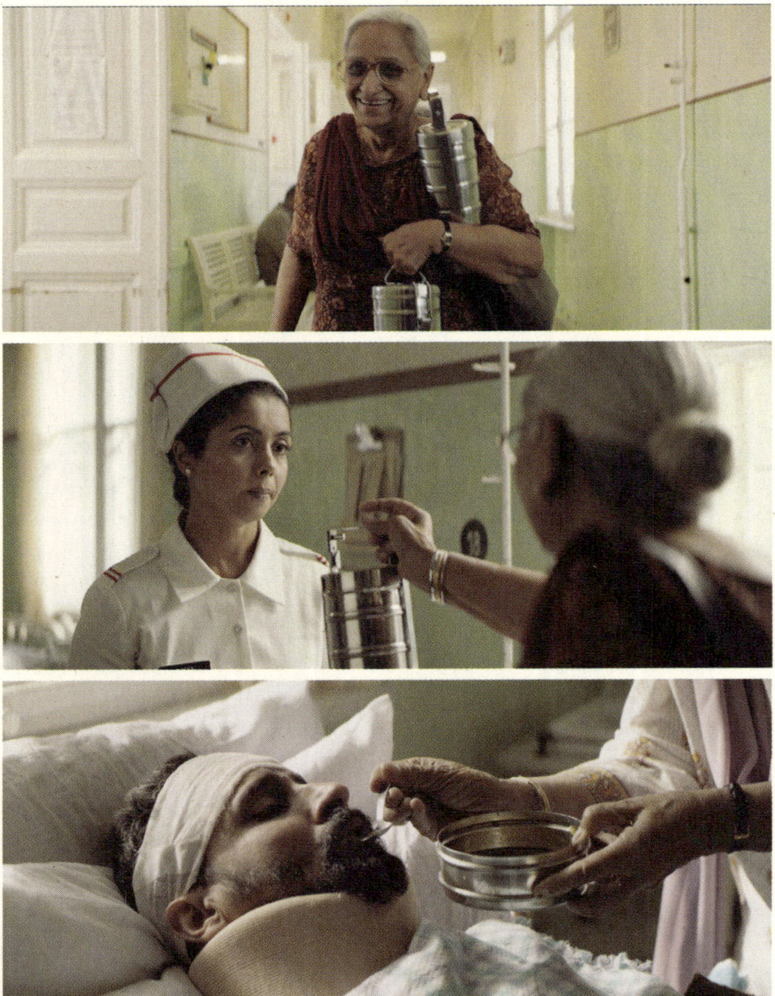

A brave client buys an ad for a cooking oil without a single shot of cooking or of the kitchen.

Now we came to the final production, and Vivek wanted to shoot in Budapest. The client was more than a little surprised. A commercial that has three characters, all Indian, set in a hospital, and you want to shoot in Budapest? I explained that we did not want to create a set; we wanted the setting to be as authentic as possible. In India, it is impossible to find an empty hospital where we could shoot, and Vivek's team had tracked down a disused army hospital in Budapest which was perfect. Of course, we underlined that the film would cost more or less the same if it had been shot in India.

Even before we completed the shoot, we knew that we had a winner. The Hungarian crew at the shoot started crying as the story revealed itself. Even though they didn't understand the language, they understood the story, thanks to the efforts of the actors. With the shoot over, it was time to edit.

It is not uncommon to find it difficult to edit something that you have shot. Every take seems important and relevant, and you do not want to discard a single shot. Vivek, Sukesh and team edited it down to five minutes and thirty seconds. I had a look and focused on points where the story dragged a bit, and had it edited again. Finally, we cut it down to four minutes and thirty-eight seconds.

We had what we thought was a great film. We had great lyrics, written by Nitin Pradhan; we now needed the music. Vivek's obsession with the film caused him to give the brief to four music directors simultaneously, and one of them delivered the magic that we wanted.

None of us involved in the film had ever created anything of this duration. The four-minute–thirty-eight-second duration would obviously make the most of the digital era; there are no additional costs for longer duration on YouTube.

Once the film was ready, we fixed up a time to show it to Pranav. On the way, I told Vivek, 'If the client loves it as much as we do, we will run it on television.' Vivek couldn't comprehend my thoughts, just thinking of the costs for TV. I explained to Vivek that in the original briefing session, I believed that this was what Pranav wanted: something so big that it would be remembered and talked about.

We presented the film without mentioning anything about its length. As the film ended, everyone in the room, including the client, had tears in their eyes. The film had done the job. It was at this point that I said that the film was four minutes, thirty-eight seconds long. At the same time, I suggested that, despite the cost, it should run at full duration for a few days on television. I offered to speak to TV channel heads to make it more financially viable.

If you take a great piece of work and combine it with the goodwill that you enjoy, great things happen. I called Anant Rangaswami of *Storyboard* on CNBC-TV18 over to see the film, and he loved it. He wanted to run it on the show (which is a weekly show that focuses on advertising, media and marketing). I agreed, with one condition—that the entire film should be run, not an excerpt. Now, it is not easy for any channel to run a four-minute–thirty-eight-second film on a programme which is twenty-three minutes long; they have many other things to cover. But *Storyboard* thought that the film deserved it and ran it in toto.

I then went to Star TV and met Sanjay Gupta. I said I have a film that is four minutes, thirty-eight seconds long. It's a beautiful film, probably one of the best pieces of work we have ever done, I said. The problem, for Star, is that they would already have sold the bulk of the inventory on prime-time shows, so there's no question of being able to fit in such a long TVC. Sanjay and executives of the cooking oil company spent ages talking to clients who had booked on various shows, requesting them to accept alternative slots. Finally, the full-length film ran on Star, on prime time.

Uday Shankar has an uncanny ability of taking bold decisions without over-intellectualizing.

Star makes investments with unwavering confidence.

While on Star, let me talk about our association with another great client, the Star TV Network. Uday Shankar, the CEO of Star, is a wonderful combination of dynamism and deep-rooted Indian values. The relaunch of Star Plus, '*Rishta Wahi, Soch Nayi*', the promotion of *Satyamev Jayate*, the launches of Life OK, the Pro Kabaddi League and the Indian Super League are some of the campaigns where I have had the opportunity of working closely with Uday and his team to help Star achieve their business ambitions. Uday has an uncanny ability of taking bold decisions without over-intellectualizing the process and then seeing it through with a confidence that is unwavering. Who could have ever imagined that kabaddi could look like an international sport? We did, and Uday was convinced that it was possible, and made all the necessary investments with his characteristic determination. It is no surprise that it is already the second most watched sport on Indian television after cricket.

I am also a big admirer of Harit Nagpal, the CEO of Tata Sky. Like Uday, Harit has a great deal of self-belief, and trusts his instincts. The body of innovations introduced by Tata Sky and the quality of creative work to communicate these innovations bear testimony to Harit's leadership abilities. The four-minute jailbreak commercial to announce the recording capability feature of Tata Sky is one example. More recently, we did an unprecedented fourteen-episode campaign which was created to promote the daily recharge offer. The serialized romantic comedy saw a daily update during IPL 8.

It is up to us to decide how involved we need to be in our work. I could have gone back to Madhukar Parekh with just another thirty-second film, as I could have with Pranav Adani. It is only when you listen carefully to briefs from your clients that you know how important a piece of communication is—and, therefore, how involved you need to be in it.

When the client is brave, one has to match the braveness, and even go beyond that. If the client is taking a risk, so must you. In both these instances, M-Seal and Fortune Cooking Oil, if the communication had failed, the reputation of the agency would have taken a beating as well.

Who would have cleared a four-minute TVC? Harit Nagpal did.

Is it worth the risk? After all, in all these cases, the income is only a fixed retainer, whether we produce a thirty-second film or a four-minute–thirty-eight-second monster. The former has little risk, while the latter is loaded with danger.

Why take the risk and not the easy way out?

It's because, when you take a risk and match the risk that your client is willing to take, both of you have a piece of the upside. The client is now more confident in you than he ever was before. The client knows that your commitment to his company goes beyond what is normally expected. And winning something together makes you a winning team—which has long-term, positive ramifications to the bottom line.

There will be times when you have a great idea, but there is a cussed brand manager who doesn't buy it. He or she forces you to do ordinary work. The client is big and important to you. But such times should not leave you disheartened. Your day will come. In the interim, remember my words, 'You can take a horse to the water, but you can't do a thing if it wants to drink piss!'

*

There's extraordinary joy in working with first-time advertisers, start-ups or companies that are getting into the consumer category for the first time.

There are also unusual challenges in these situations, especially in the need to educate the clients, and getting them to feel comfortable and confident about the communication.

Amara Raja wasn't a start-up; it was a successful, profitable company manufacturing industrial batteries—essentially a B2B firm. They were now foraying into automotive batteries with their consumer-facing brand, Amaron, for the first time; this meant that they needed to advertise the product for the first time.

For the automotive-battery business, Amara Raja had set up a joint venture with Johnson Controls Inc., one of the largest manufacturers of batteries globally. In addition to the technical expertise that Johnson Controls brought to the table, they were also extremely design oriented, so we were dealing with a high-quality product that also looked good.

There's extraordinary joy in working with first-time advertisers such as Amaron.

Every positive attribute helped, as the largest in the category was Exide, a brand that was almost generic to automotive batteries.

The client, Jay Galla, gave us a free rein which, as I have said before, adds a lot of pressure. When the trust levels are so high, one feels the weight of the responsibility. Perhaps the responsibility led us to cautious, functional, almost boring ideas—till we told ourselves that conventional advertising would not help a new brand that was fighting a behemoth like Exide.

On the surface of it, batteries are as boring a category as one could imagine. You rarely ever get to see the battery as it is hidden under the bonnet of a car or tucked into a compartment in a two-wheeler. The only time you see the battery is when it stops working.

The creative team handling the campaign decided to embark on a route that would do just the opposite—drive attention to the battery, make the battery seem cool, and make the communication fun. Since one of the rational selling propositions was the long life of the battery, the campaign centred on this aspect. This was hardly an unusual promise in battery advertising. What was different was how we treated the campaign, using clay animation for the first time in advertising in India. The script, the clay animation figures and the voice-over made batteries friendlier and 'less functional'.

To me, there was a huge similarity between Fevicol and Amaron, because both are, by and large, invisible products. Fevicol disappears into the furniture that your carpenter builds for you, and the Amaron battery is tucked away in the recesses of your vehicle. Be it Fevicol, Amaron, M-Seal or other low-involvement category products, the route to making the consumer more involved was to talk less about the functional aspects of the product and focus more on making the product a friend.

It is easy to dismiss a category as boring, and once you do so, it will be almost impossible to get consumers excited about the category itself, let alone the brand.

I've always believed that no category is a boring category; you have to stare hard at the product and the brand, and discover how exciting you can make it. For example, what could be exciting about a 50 cc moped? That's what Luna was. Our '*Chal Meri Luna*' campaign made the Luna, which is hardly a Harley Davidson, cool and aspirational.

I've always believed that no category is a boring category—and neither is a brand.

When younger colleagues dismiss a product as boring, I remind them of Fevicol. If Fevicol, an adhesive used by carpenters, can be interesting, any category can be interesting.

Brands like Amaron, Fevicol, M-Seal and Luna presented some unique challenges and opportunities, but so did a global, established brand like Kentucky Fried Chicken when they first came to India.

KFC, as everyone in advertising knew, was 'Finger Lickin' Good', and, expectedly from a multinational, they wanted us to take the international campaigns and rehash them for India.

We felt we had to bring some meaning into the line 'Finger Lickin' Good'. The way the line was being used in the markets where KFC had been present for some years, it was just three words tucked away near the KFC logo.

I've always believed that no category is a boring category; you have to stare hard at the product and the brand, and discover how exciting you can make it.

We decided to target the young, modern, westward-looking and experimental audience. As a result, we had to get away from all the expected and predictable routes to advertise food. We presented a series of print ads to establish 'Finger Lickin' Good' with visuals of hands, with the headline 'Cutlery at KFC' and the line 'Finger Lookin' Good' prominently near the KFC logo.

The campaign was rooted in a very simple insight—no one in India ate chicken only with cutlery. At some point, the chicken piece is picked up in your hands, forcing you to lick your fingers.

Even as we rolled out with the campaign, we had to bear in mind that among the most difficult things to change are the food habits of any country. 'Cutlery at KFC' was the first step in the strategy to create a buzz with the youth, because we didn't think that we could convert samosa and kachori lovers into embracing KFC, nor could we drive the tandoori chicken-eating taxi drivers to an American fried-chicken outlet.

We used a lot of cricket in the early period of KFC in India. For example, we did a radio campaign with Chetan Shashital, mimicking Sachin's voice, saying, 'I hate ducks, ducks don't look good on a scoreboard,' followed by a long discourse on why he hated ducks. Finally, after the duck rant, the voice says, 'That's why I love chicken, particularly at KFC.'

The largest and most successful campaign for KFC also used cricket. We made a TVC that featured Muttiah Muralitharan, the

Sri Lankan spinner, showing him wetting his fingers with saliva (as he did while bowling), and getting transported to the memory of eating chicken at KFC.

That one campaign resulted in sales shooting through the roof, and Muktesh Pant, the then CEO of Yum Foods, and Niren Chaudhary who heads it today, presented us with a diary, saying, 'The first chapter in KFC's history in India has been written by you; now fill the diary.'

That'll take some filling up, as KFC has almost 400 outlets in the country today.

It's easy when one works with an established brand, to just rehash the work done in other markets—but that can also be suicidal. When we won the KFC account, we looked at the brand in the context of the Indian market, Indian habits and Indian insights.

We looked at KFC as we looked at Amaron. We wanted the brand to be loved, we wanted the brand to entertain and we wanted the brand to challenge the status quo.

Then there is the story of an international client who created advertising in India for the first time—Perfetti Van Melle. The rock star here was an ex-Hindustan Lever man: Ashok Dhingra. Ashok and his colleague Sameer Suneja had stuck their necks out, convincing the head office of the need to create communication in India, for India. Ashok first met me in Delhi and enthused me to no end. He said, 'Yes, I was in Hindustan Lever but not in marketing, so don't fear me.' He then added, 'We make delightful products, so give me delightful advertising.' Ashok and Sameer, who went on to become the Worldwide CEO of Perfetti, delighted Team Ogilvy and me for over a decade. Over the years, we have worked on great brands such as Center Fresh, Center Fruit, Alpenliebe Lollipop, Mentos, Center Shock, Sour Marbles, and so on. I remember once Ashok and Sameer walking into my office with a jar of gum candy called Center Shock. They said, 'We have made a great product, now you make a great campaign.' This was the one-line brief!

Ashok Dhingra wanted delightful advertising—and that's what we gave him.

I tasted the product; it was so sour that it shook me up. I said the line for this is, '*Hilake Rakh de*'—'It will shake the hell out of you'. They said, 'Great! Now you write the commercial and we are going ahead with the distribution with the label 'Center Shock, Hilake Rakh de'. I wish there were more people like them.

Later, Abhijit created the famous barber commercial which shook the country. Mentos '*Dimaag ki Batti Jala de*' has become iconic. The journey continues, as more creative people in Ogilvy Bombay and Delhi want to work with Perfetti. I am sure so do people at McCann who handle some of the Perfetti brands.

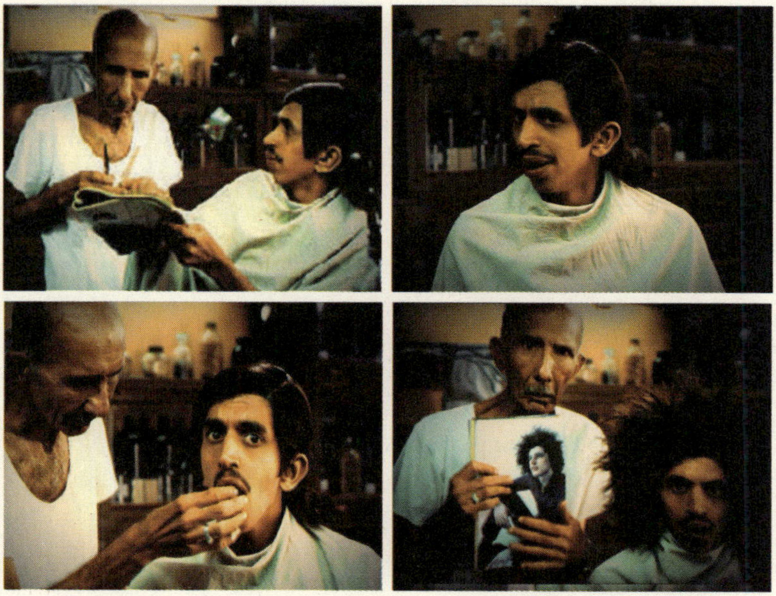

Just a one-line brief: 'We have made a great product, now you make a great campaign.'

12

'Lala' Is Not a Four-letter Word

There are a lot of negative perceptions about family-owned businesses, often referred to as 'lala' companies, and how difficult they are as clients. Over the decades, I've dealt with several of them, and I find them as easy or as difficult to deal with as any other professional company.

Nita Ambani has been a client many times over. When she has a remit, she takes it seriously and is very hands-on. So, when we deal with her as the owner of Mumbai Indians, do we deal with a 'family' business? Mrs Ambani wants Mumbai Indians, the team she owns, to do well, as much as any CEO of any company would want his or her company to excel; similarly, she wants to build a strong brand, she wants the brand to be spoken about, to increase in value . . . She also wants outstanding communication. What she wants is no different from what any professional CEO would want and should want.

She doesn't run a family business; she runs a business like a family, that's the difference.

When my team and I go for meetings with her, it's immediately apparent that, as a good manager, she wants the whole team to be comfortable before the meeting begins. On an average, there would be seven or eight colleagues at every such meeting. Mrs Ambani will approach each of them, call them by their names, urging them to have snacks and tea or coffee before the meeting begins. She will ensure that everybody is comfortable and in a relaxed state of mind before we get down to business.

Nita Ambani has a strong opinion that she expresses, as is the right of every client. But, as with every good client, she listens carefully to our opinions as well. Importantly, she understands that each and every team member has a good reason to be in the meeting, so she listens to every single opinion.

Her attitude is simple: she is dealing with professionals who know their jobs and their responsibilities, irrespective of their age and gender. As a result, it could be the juniormost member from my team who narrates a script; she understands and respects that.

What she does differently (when compared to non-'lala' clients) is to add an element to a professional meeting that we rarely see nowadays—*khaatirdari*. It's a wonderful Hindi word, almost impossible to translate, but I'll try anyway. It's great, genuine hospitality, coming from the heart, intended to make guests feel that they are special, unique and wanted.

Old mindsets believe that professional companies are better than the so-called family companies.

If that is something you get from 'lala' clients, I'll take that any day. Perhaps, it's something all of us should learn from Mrs Ambani—to take the edge of transaction out of professional meetings.

While a lot of agencies are wary of dealing with family businesses, Ogilvy has revelled in them. Much of the wariness comes from not understanding the truth that family-run businesses and professionalism are not mutually exclusive. We've done some of our best work, whether judged for creativity or for effectiveness, with family-run businesses.

Take a look at our basket: Mumbai Indians, obviously; then we have Madhukar Parekh and Pidilite; Ashwin Dani and Asian Paints; the Birlas, Godrej, Bajaj, Dabur. The list can go on and on.

When we try and motivate our colleagues to be more passionate about a brand, we often say, 'Believe that you own the brand.' In other words, we are saying that the person who owns the brand is the one who is the most passionate about it. If this is the case, wouldn't the brand owner be the gold standard for passion? Talk to Rajiv Bajaj and you will understand why I say that. If Rajiv Bajaj was to be reborn, he would like to be born as a motorcycle.

If Rajiv Bajaj was to be reborn, he would like to be born as a motorcycle.

Asian Paints, the super-professional family-run company.

All these companies go beyond professionalism—and they add a personal and warm touch to cold business relationships. Let me share a story about Bharat Puri, a story that could never be told by a 'professional' company.

Bharat Puri was the blue-eyed boy of Asian Paints when he received, and accepted, an offer from Cadbury. Ashwin Dani decided to throw a farewell party at his house for Bharat; you would say that's normal. What was not normal was what was on the schedule immediately preceding the party.

Dani had organized a puja to bless Bharat with good fortune as he left Asian Paints for Cadbury. That is what was unusual. That was magical. In 'professional' companies, farewell parties are common. But a puja to wish an employee who is leaving the company? That demonstrates heart; that demonstrates a generosity that is so rare and refreshing. Most importantly, it's something that 'professional' companies do not do, and that's unfortunate. Bharat Puri might have forgotten many farewell parties, but the puja at Ashwin Dani's house is an experience he will remember all his life.

There's a huge difference in the way that family-run businesses are run when compared to what we call 'professional' companies. Family-run companies are more sensitive, and demonstrate more warmth and sensitivity. That's what leads to their amazing ability to retain talent. Senior executives are able to see their value beyond their salary slips; when they know that they are wanted and they know that their views are respected, and they know that the company they work for is sensitive to their needs and concerns, they are less inclined to jump jobs. It's no surprise then that even these days, we see many family-run companies enjoying the advantage of continuity in leadership and an extraordinarily high level of loyalty. There is, of course, an extraordinary amount of control—at least the perception of control. That brings me to the most important point: which company, family-run or otherwise, does not exercise control?

Nita Ambani wants just what any 'professional' CEO would: Outstanding communication.

Which company isn't a 'lala' company? Which 'professional' listed company isn't a 'lala' company? Isn't WPP a 'lala' company with Sir Martin Sorrell as the 'lala', even if it is a listed, traded company? Isn't he our 'lala' sitting at the WPP HQ in London? Why don't we equate Martin Sorrell with Nita Ambani? Or, Maurice Levy with Kumaramangalam Birla?

Old mindsets believe that professional companies are better than the so-called family companies. It's when you know that Pidilite Industries Ltd, the family-run company, had a market valuation of Rs 27,837 crore as on 31 March 2014 that you realize the fallacy of the statement.

I could go on and on listing the various family-run businesses that we have had the privilege of working with. Siddhee Cement and Haathi Cement of Jay Mehta, Onida with Gulu Mirchandani. TBZ is another example.

Look at the continuity in Ogilvy's relationships with family-run businesses. Some of these are forty years old, some thirty years, and so on. That's the biggest advantage of doing good work for family-owned businesses. As they do with their employees, so they do with their business partners: they reward hard work and loyalty.

We see the family-run businesses as great clients. What makes them more interesting is that they continue to stay entrepreneurial as they grow, resetting their own challenges and, consequently, the challenges that we are tasked with addressing.

This brings me to a personal failure. In all these years, we haven't worked with one of the finest family-run businesses in India; we've never worked with Anand Mahindra.

That's not a family-run business anyone will walk away from; most ad agencies would give an arm and a leg to handle a piece of the Mahindra Group's business.

13

Sorry, It's Not Enough to Be Multinational

We often use the adjective 'multinational' to describe companies, and I'm amazed by the continued use. Ogilvy being 'multinational' means very little to brands that we work for, or to the consumer—all it means is that Ogilvy has offices in many countries. 'Multinational', for me, fails to capture the essential advantage that being present in many countries allows: that we become 'multicultural'. If we add the descriptor 'multicultural' to 'multinational', making it 'multicultural multinational', the benefits to our clients and to consumers is immediately visible. The phrase 'immediately visible' suggests that, in addition to our being physically present in many countries, we also understand the cultures of these countries, and that we have local insights; we can tell stories in all these countries which will immediately connect with the local consumers.

It's easy to be multinational. Being truly multicultural is harder. What is entertaining in one's country can be offensive in another. What is edgy in one's country might be quite normal in another. The drivers for the purchase of biscuits in one country differ from the drivers in another. All these differences are because of different cultures, not because of different geographies.

Ogilvy is multicultural—because we work hard at it.

All multinational companies, I feel, should change their nomenclature to multicultural companies. Multinational is the statement of the owner, the statement of the speaker, to say that the company has a presence in so many countries. Multicultural is the statement of a receiver to say somebody understands his or her culture. There is a huge difference; multinational is an up-to-down way of looking at life, while multicultural is a down-to-up way of looking at life.

Multicultural is a statement of humility. It says that the company is not the king, the consumer is the king. Over the years, Ogilvy has been a multicultural company that follows this belief; it's a multicultural company that unites rather than dictates.

This redefinition questions designations such as 'regional head'. I'd prefer 'cultural head', a position that works closely with cultural partners, with insights and knowledge of other cultures; imagine if we redesignated someone as Cultural Partner, Dove, or as Cultural Partner, Coca-Cola, and so on; it would change the way we think of the brand, the business, the environment and, of course, the consumer.

Multicultural is a statement of humility. It says that the company is not the king, the consumer is the king.

To be responsible to different cultures, one needs to ensure that nothing is taken for granted. In India, for example, if your daughter came to meet me, it is normal and expected of me to pat her on the head and say, 'Beta, God bless you.'

It is part of our culture.

In some other country, in another culture, my patting a little girl might cause great offence. That's when I would need a cultural partner there who tells me, 'Piyush, in this culture, your patting a child's head is unacceptable.'

The understanding that we live and operate in a multicultural world is essential for every single multinational company—so that no unintentional offence is caused.

India and Pakistan were one nation sixty-eight years ago, and we could presume that we know each other well. We might, but never well enough to take it for granted. As recently as a couple of years ago, a youngster from the Delhi office designed the Ogilvy signature logo in Urdu, and his senior, Ajay Gahlaut, shared the idea with me.

It was a fantastic graphic. It closely resembled the English logo that we use, and I asked Ajay to go to a Muslim university, meet a professor who is an expert in Urdu, and ask him to confirm that the Urdu was absolutely perfect and that there was nothing culturally offensive in the graphic treatment. I also insisted that the professor certify that the treatment was okay. Ajay identified an authority, shared the logo with him and returned with the certificate.

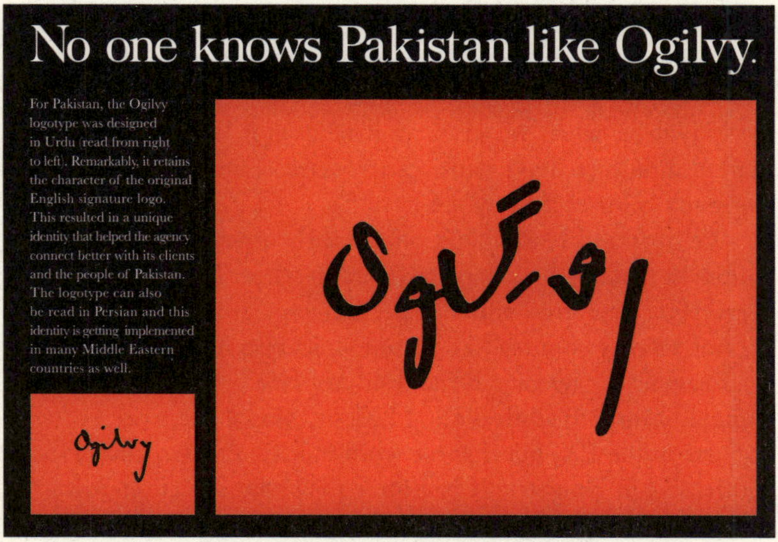

Extreme care needs to be taken about multicultural and multinational issues.

Since it was both a multicultural and a multinational issue, the matter didn't end there. I sent the logo and the certificate to my Pakistan office, asking them to conduct a similar exercise with experts in Pakistan. Only after the local experts certified the logo, were we satisfied and confident that the work was culturally aligned, and we changed our identity in Urdu-speaking countries with this logo.

It's in thinking of ourselves as multicultural that caused us to be sensitive to local thoughts, views, opinions, trends, tastes and fashion. This sensitivity does not come from being multinational.

Try it out. Change the way you think of your company. Once you see yourself as multicultural, you'll be more accepted and loved. To top it, you will sell more toothpastes, soaps, shampoos, cars, mobile phones, chocolates and, of course, advertising.

The concept of multiculturalism is easily extended within the country as well. If one says that Ogilvy is a 'national agency', it immediately suggests that we have offices across the country.

That is a quantitative rather than a qualitative statement. The suggestion that we have offices in Mumbai, Gurgaon, Kolkata, and so on, is information of little value to anyone.

Nowhere, when we say 'national' does it lead to the thought that, in addition to having offices across the country, we understand the many cultures that we see in India.

We hear and read, many times, of the premise that India is a continent and not a country; a continent where food habits change every 100 kilometres; where dialects change every 100 kilometres. It's not an easy country to do communication in.

Imagine an agency being told to create just one piece of communication to address all of Europe. Maybe the work becomes popular in the UK, but doesn't work in, say, Poland, and perhaps is offensive in Hungary. If you force the communication down the throats of these people, you will be the loser. The same is true of India. It's all but impossible to create that one piece of communication that works across the country.

India is such a diverse country with so many languages, so many cultures, so many dialects, so many food habits, so many expressions of music, so many expressions of dancing, that the work we do should recognize these realities.

The diversity is both challenging and amazing. In Kolkata, mustard oil is used for cooking. In Mumbai, people are aghast at the thought of cooking in mustard oil; they massage their scalps with it. Everything in Rajasthan is cooked in pure ghee, and that's abhorrent to many other cultures. When a Rajasthani visits Kerala, he is stunned that the very same coconut oil that he uses on his hair is used in cooking the fish that he is eating.

The beautiful challenge in India is to search for, and find, the unity in this diversity. You have to look for those tastes, behaviours and thoughts that are common, and which unify all these cultures. Every once in a while, we do find such elements, and that is when the resultant communication moves consumers.

14

A Captain Is Only as Good as the Team

Those who are into cricket will agree that the sheer brilliance of Brian Lara could not make the West Indies win matches. Purely because he did not have a great team like Clive Lloyd did. I am no Brian Lara, but I have always had a great team.

Over the years, one of the biggest exaggerations is that I am involved in every piece of communication that leaves the Ogilvy office. This myth gets underlined each time the agency produces work that is clutter-breaking, hugely popular or wins awards.

Those who are unconnected with the agency will miraculously find a 'Piyush touch' in some elements or the other of the communication, even when I have had absolutely no direct contribution to the work.

Take Vodafone, for example. My biggest contribution to the excellent work on the brand is the fact that I have never got involved in any creative directly, leaving it to V. Mahesh and Rajiv Rao, and after the unfortunate and tragic death of Mahesh, to Rajiv. My involvement in Vodafone is to be a sounding board to Rajiv when he needs one, to look at the work at critical stages and to offer constructive criticism when I feel the need.

The Google film: A beautiful piece of work in which I had no role to play.

This is true of many accounts. Competent teams do the heavy lifting, while I am available when required. Now, take a beautiful piece of work, where it is easier to believe I had no role to play: the 'Google Reunion Search' film. Anyone who knows me is aware of the fact that I do not use the computer, so how on earth would I know the nuances of Google and be able to leverage them? Yet, there are many who see the sensitivity and emotion in the film and say that's 'the Piyush touch'.

The truth of the matter is that it is Sukesh Nayak, Abhijit Awasthi and their teams who created the film; my first involvement was when I saw the film. The next contribution was to tell the team to ensure that they had a great track to lift the already brilliant film even higher. Immediately after the film became a runaway hit, many said that the track must have been written by me. Again, I had nothing to do with it; the entire credit goes to its creator, Nilesh Jain. Thank God I was not involved in the film; Sukesh and Abhijit were inspired and charged, and the director was on a roll. The team was so confident that they didn't care about the unusual length and, finally, the client was so overjoyed that he bought the concept in its entirety and supported it strongly.

In instances such as this, I get angry because I feel it is dangerous. If those who deserve the credit and recognition do not get it, they could so easily get demotivated. That's why I am quick to set the record straight, loud and clear, in public. It's easier to do so today when we have so many media publications that write about advertising, but it wasn't always so. For example, while I certainly wrote '*Har ghar kuch keheta hai*' for Asian Paints, I did not write the next one, which is even more beautiful. The line is '*Iss ghar mein rotiyaan kabhi ginn ke nahi banti*'. Many people started congratulating me for it and I was apologetically insisting that I had nothing to do with it. It was written by Shekhar Jha.

Over time, the moment we produced something brilliant in Hindi, everyone presumed it was my work. The moment it is Hindi, the moment it is emotional, a lot of people tend to believe it is Piyush. There is only so much that I am capable of; the magic of Ogilvy is that there are a whole lot of people who remember brilliant stories from their own experience and use them to create extraordinary advertising for the brands we work on.

Perceptions can also cause one to make bad decisions—and lose out on possibilities. For example, in the early days of my career, if a boy in the creative team had a surname, like, for example, De Souza, I wouldn't have trusted him with a brand that needed communication in Hindi and would have suggested that he work on a brand like Lakme.

If I am not scoring runs like my partners are, then I shouldn't be in the team.

Think of what I would have done: passed a judgement on the capability of a young creative based solely on his name. It didn't take me too long to learn to reject the name, the physical characteristics, the gender and the regional roots of my colleagues, and to embrace their knowledge and talent alone. Not surprising then that we have a Ryan Mendonca who wrote '*Bournvita tayyari jeet ki*' and we have a Zenobia Pithawalla writing the brilliant '*Bell Bajao*' campaign.

I get surprised every day by a colleague who might be Bengali or Malayali, yet narrating a brilliant script in Hindi. Sometimes, their accents may cause me to guffaw, but their insights and use of language surprise me pleasantly.

I could devote an entire book to correcting perceptions, giving credit where it's due and sharing with you details of the numerous talented individuals who make Ogilvy the great agency that it is. *Ogilvy is not Piyush Pandey, never was and never will be.* Ogilvy is the sum of many Abhijits, Rajivs, Ajays, Zenobias, Prasoons, Bobbys, Anils, Sonals, Sukeshs and Sumantos who have worked here for whatever period of time. And of course, the many Piyushs.

All I have believed is that unlike tennis, in advertising there is no such thing as a non-playing captain. So, I write and think of ideas like every other creative director does. If I am not scoring runs like my partners are, then I shouldn't be in the team. And if you are not in the team, how can you be the captain? Like Clive Lloyd, I also score some runs for the team, but then it doesn't mean I score all the runs. I have my Vivian Richardses, Gordon Greenidges, and a battery of fast bowlers.

15

Step Out of the Crease

My mother used to say, '*Mujhe ghoomne ka bahut shauk hai*' (I like to travel), and I would say, '*Mujhe ghumaane ka bahut shauk hai*' (I like to make people travel). I have recommended strange places to my good friends Madhukar and Mala Parekh (of Pidilite), and they actually went there.

It's no surprise then that Ogilvy India has done more tourism advertising than anyone else. We launched the 'Incredible India' campaign (for India Tourism) which made waves around the world. It was a great piece of work done by my colleague, V. Sunil, and his team.

We launched Madhya Pradesh Tourism under the leadership of Yashodhara Raje Scindia, then tourism minister of the state. Again, it was a fantastic initiative of putting MP on the map of preferred destinations. We had huge financial constraints on the production of the films, as the MP Tourism department had not budgeted for an advertising campaign. We came up with the idea of a bioscope; we did no video shooting at all, instead, we used existing still photographs and post-production techniques which eventually delighted the hearts of the consumer.

Then I had a fantastic personal experience of working on a state which I had not known much about at a deeper and cultural level. This was Gujarat. The man behind the campaign was Mr Narendra Modi (then chief minister of Gujarat, now Prime Minister of India). His officer in charge of tourism was Vipul Mittra. The brand ambassador was and is Mr Amitabh Bachchan. I was briefed on the vision for the state and the details of each destination by Mr Modi himself. I don't think I have been briefed more thoroughly by any client in my life. He spoke and he spoke and he spoke. And then he said, 'Don't listen to me so much, I won't stop. You have to say it in just sixty seconds.' It was a humbling experience. I said, 'Sir, you keep talking. I will pick up what will make for a sixty-second commercial.'

We had the privilege of working on the Incredible India campaign since inception.

In the next four years, I got a lesson in communication. Between Mr Bachchan, my team and me, Vipul Mittra, and Shoojit Sircar and his team, we saw Gujarat fairly well. Jungles of Gir, the port of Porbandar, Ahmedabad, religious places like Dwarka, Somnath and Siddhpur. I never knew that Siddhpur is the only revered place for one's mother's *shraadh* (final rites). Nor did Mr Bachchan. We both performed the rites for our respective mothers after the shoot.

Imagine how much my young team and I learnt about India from this experience. We then went on to do campaigns for Jammu and Kashmir Tourism, Daman and Diu, and Dadra and Nagar Haveli Tourism. These were great opportunities for my team to know and feel the people of India. The campaign for Daman and

My mother used to say, '*Mujhe ghoomne ka bahut shauk hai*' (I like to travel), and I would say, '*Mujhe ghumaane ka bahut shauk hai*' (I like to make people travel).

Diu, and Dadra and Nagar Haveli, is a result of a creative team wanting to do things differently and a brave client backing it to the hilt. 'Ilha de Calma', or the Island of Calm, is not something that a bureaucrat buys easily. Yet, the administrator Ashish Kundra backed the campaign and ran it with enough frequency for the world to take notice. This unique concept created by Sumanto Chattopadhyay and his team was brilliantly picturized by Prakash Varma and his team at Nirvana. A lot of my colleagues who had read geography in their childhood and believed that Goa, Daman and Diu were next to each other realized that all union territories were not next to each other. Even I got to see Daman for the first time in my life. Those of my colleagues who had the opportunity of working on Jammu and Kashmir Tourism and on the campaign for the North-eastern states are now more enlightened about their country than ever before. As this is being written, we have been assigned the work for Rajasthan Tourism, something that I have waited for thirty-three years in advertising. I will now have the pleasure of taking my team on a baby walk on my own turf.

Now we are working for Chhattisgarh Tourism. Young men and women of my team are engaging with the people of Chhattisgarh, travelling with them, seeing India like never before and learning every day. Isn't it nice to step out of the crease and play?

Working on Gujarat Tourism was a lesson in communication.

Tourism businesses are opportunities to know and feel the people of India.

Diu is an opportunity for great print and TV ads.

My tourism account bug: 'Mujhe ghumaane ka bahut shauk hai' *(I like to make people travel).*

16

Don't Forget Where You Came From

It has been forty-three years since I stopped living in Jaipur, but whenever I'm in need of an idea, I go back to where I came from. The house that I grew up in was visited by all kinds of people; young, old, neighbours, doctors, friends, relatives—and without appointments or informing us earlier. These unannounced visits could be at all times of the day, including mealtimes, and my mother would always welcome all visitors warmly. I do the same thing in Bombay, because in the open house that my mother ran, I learnt of the sensitivity of relationships. Whenever something that I write touches people, it's because of the way that relationships are portrayed—and my writing is based on the relationships that I saw in my house in Jaipur.

Some of my classmates from school are still in Jaipur. Many others, like me, have moved to other cities. We have, naturally, achieved various levels of success and have lived very different lives over these years. But when we meet, we try to turn the clock back, doing the same things we did when we first became friends, such as visiting the same kachoriwallah, and so on. My brother Prasoon, on a trip to Jaipur with his family, wanted his children to see and experience the Jaipur of his childhood. He hired a cycle rickshaw for the day, rode the rickshaw himself and took the kids to all the places that he loved and remembered, and introduced them to people whom he knew.

Times may change, but relationships don't—and you can rediscover the nuances of old relationships and experiences by revisiting the place where you first encountered them.

I don't wear India on my sleeve. I wear it on my heart. No, I am not a jingoistic nationalist, but I am proud to be an Indian. My mother used to say, 'Get to know your neighbour, otherwise you won't get to know the world.' I have always taken this advice seriously. I have tried to see as much of India as I could. I know there is a lot more to see. I have tried to understand the different Indian cultures. I know I have to try harder, but the hunger is there.

Travelling the world, knowing about different countries, their people and culture, is a beautiful experience. I have loved every bit of it, but I have never had the desire to live anywhere else but India. There have been several proposals made to me to move countries, all well intended, but I have never been happy about the idea.

Play where you can make a difference. Not just to yourself, but also to a large number of your community, your country.

I still remember when I went through a divorce in the early nineties. Mani Ayer, my managing director, was concerned about what I was going through. He found an opportunity for me to be Ogilvy's ECD in Malaysia. He even went to the extent of finding cricket clubs in Kuala Lumpur where I could pursue my interest. I almost accepted, but then God saved me as the opportunity disappeared. Since then, there have been times when I have had an offer from Ogilvy to do a regional job out of Singapore. I didn't accept it. I was told by my colleagues that if I didn't do an international assignment, how would I be known internationally? I said jokingly, 'I will sit in India and hoist the Indian flag internationally.'

In 2004, when I was asked to be the president of the jury for Films, Press and Poster at the Cannes Advertising Festival, it was a first for an Asian in fifty years.

It is useful to reach out to the world and learn new things. Unfortunately, most of those who go abroad, don't come back to apply their learning in India. There is so much Indian talent that resides outside India. I hope they can come back to contribute when the country is poised for great things.

Advertising, too, has lost a lot of talent to Singapore, the UK and the US. I am sorry to say that barring one, all have disappeared from the scene. They did not do any significant work there and now they are insignificant back in India. These are harsh words, but true.

Play where you can make a difference. Not just to yourself, but also to a large number of those in your community, your country. On a lighter note, I didn't go out because nobody makes better food than Indians. There is no better food in the world when compared with the food available on the dining table of Indian families.

3

SO MUCH COMPLEXITY IS FOUND IN SIMPLICITY

17

Standing Up for One's Beliefs

I have been brought up to stand up for my beliefs, for my point of view and what I think is right. It's not always been easy to do so because if you stand up for your views that conflict with those of your seniors or your clients, your neck would most certainly be on the line.

This difference of opinion is not rebellion or disrespect—it's only deep conviction that your view is better, or more apt. It can happen with a father and a son or a father and a daughter, when the child feels that there is a better way to deal with something. If the child is completely convinced, it could also stand up against the parent. But how can one argue without appearing to be both disrespectful and rebellious?

In a creative profession, this is a situation one faces often, especially in the early stages of one's career. How does a rookie argue with a creative director or a branch head or a marketing director?

However difficult it may be, if you are convinced that you are right, then you should stand up for your beliefs. Having said that, one has to deal with the situation with sensitivity, tact and confidence.

Much will depend on the impact that your confidence and conviction can make on your audience.

*

The 'Tiger Pataudi' campaign was in a way the Zoozoo of those days. We created multiple ads. In each of them, Tiger Pataudi made pre-match comments on the next day's game. He talked about the state of the pitch, the history of the matches played at a particular ground and tactics that might help. The ads looked like live commercials. We went to the extent of shooting two options for the final. In option one, Tiger began with 'Great, India made it to the final', while in option two he began with 'Alas, India did not make it to the final'.

The brand was Phillips PHX, and Mr Nobi Gupta, one of India's most recognized marketing professionals, was the client. It's tougher when the difference of opinion is with a mentor of your immediate seniors, as was the case with a pitch campaign for Tata Cement. In the early nineties, the team led by me worked on what we thought was a great campaign for over a month, and we were really convinced that we would win. Before the presentation to the client, we had to showcase the work to our own strategy review board, comprising Mani Ayer, Roda Mehta and Suresh Mullick, which oversaw all work that was considered important to the agency. Normally, the work would have been reviewed at an earlier stage, but for reasons I cannot quite remember, this review was put off till just a couple of days before the presentation to the client.

However difficult it may be, if you are convinced that you are right, then you should stand up for your beliefs.

When we presented the work to the board, it was rejected as rubbish. In fact, they believed that the work was so poor that it was way beyond repair, and that we would have to go back to the drawing board. I was livid; here was a group of people who had passed judgement on work that they had no involvement in, rejecting what my team and I were immersed in, and believed in intensely. Worse, none of them had seen the work-in-progress over the past month and the consequent iterations. If any of the board members had been involved from the outset, we wouldn't have been in this sorry state.

Seething, I told the board that if the work was rejected, I rejected the rejection. I walked out of the room and went back home. The board members thought this was an impulsive reaction and that I would calm down and return. I didn't. Suresh called me on the phone a number of times, telling me that certain aspects of the campaign were good, suggesting that I meet them halfway and make modifications.

I refused to budge because of my conviction that we had created a campaign that would work brilliantly.

Finally, Suresh called, saying Mani wanted to meet me. I went to the office thinking that I was being sacked. Mani and I had a brief conversation. All he said was, 'If you're so convinced, we'll go ahead with it.'

Of course, what was unsaid was that I would be history if we didn't win the pitch.

We finally went for the pitch with no change. When we reached Tata Cement, we learnt that we would be the last but one (out of nine agencies) to present. As soon as we finished our presentation, Aditya Kashyap, the managing director of this new company called Tata Cement, walked up to me, gave me a hug and said, 'The business is yours.' I understand that the pitch stopped with our presentation; Aditya didn't want to see any of the remaining presentations.

To Mani Ayer's credit, he never held the incident against me, and he never gave me the impression that he believed that I had rebelled. On the contrary, he magnanimously said, 'The boy was right.' In hindsight, I'd say that he started respecting me more after this incident.

The Tata Cement pitch only reinforced my belief that, if one is convinced about an issue, one has to stand by the conviction. I could have been sacked, and considering the stature of Ogilvy and of the members on the review board, being sacked would possibly mean that I would never again get a job in advertising.

But the upside? I won an account for the agency. My conviction in my work got me noticed by Mani Ayer. Perhaps the Tata Cement win was a turning point in my career at Ogilvy and in my life as a creative professional.

18

Look Back at Life, There Are Stories Hidden There

Whenever I feel bereft of ideas or hit a block, I find inspiration by rewinding life to my childhood and going back to my formative years. That's when the mind was pure, unafraid, unconstructed and unfettered. In this phase of life, gems are hidden, and that's where I go to look for them.

What can a crazy outing with college friends contribute to my advertising career? Lots, as this story will tell you.

A group of friends from St. Stephen's College—Digvijay Singh, then the head of Zee TV, Rajiv Agarwal who was running his own ad agency—a few others and I made a plan to go on a boat ride from the Gateway of India, directly opposite the Taj Mahal hotel in Bombay. Digvijay, Rajiv and I rode to the Gateway in the same car. When we reached there, we discovered that there was no free parking space. (One could park opposite the Gateway then, something we cannot do post-26/11.)

I told Digvijay and Rajiv to wait in the car while I 'created' a parking space. I walked around till I noticed a car with a chauffeur seated at the wheel, and noted down its registration number. I went back to Digvijay and told him to keep an eye on that particular spot, as the car would move out in the next few minutes. I walked across to the Taj portico and asked them to call for the car with the registration number that I had just noted down. The car approached in a couple of minutes, and I slipped away unnoticed. By the time I reached the Gateway, Digvijay had parked our car in the spot that I had just got vacated.

Twenty-five years later, I converted the memory of this experience into a Sprite commercial.

That's where many ideas for many brands can be found—in the recesses of your memory. A lot of my stories are inspired by memories of incidents with family, friends, colleagues, or simple observations.

An experience with friends transformed into a Sprite commercial.

One of the ads that gave me a lot of recognition and touched a lot of hearts was an ad for SBI Life, about a senior citizen gifting his wife a diamond.

Way back when my brother Prasoon and I had started working, and had managed to save a little bit of money, we wanted to buy a present for our mother. But we couldn't figure out what she would like. One of our sisters mentioned that she had never had a diamond (she obviously had other jewellery), so we bought her a pair of diamond earrings. When we presented them to her, she started crying and said, 'What will I do with diamonds at this age?' Her reaction was the inspiration for the SBI Life commercial.

Old age is a source for discovering purity.

There are many commercials which are inspired by my memories of my mother. My mother was very keen to complete the '*Chaar Dhaam*', the pilgrimage of the four holy sites at Badrinath, Dwarka, Puri and Rameswaram. She had been to three, but had not been to

Dwarka. My sister Ila travelled with her to Dwarka, via Jamnagar, the closest airport. They had hired a car to go from the airport to the temple, only to discover that the last couple of kilometres were not motorable (in those days). My mother, then more than eighty years old, was in no shape to walk the distance, so Ila had to look for another solution. She spotted a vegetable vendor with a cart built like a large tricycle. She asked him how much he would charge for the entire cartload of vegetables. He named a figure. Ila then proposed that she pay him that sum and let him keep the vegetables if he emptied his cart and allowed her to ferry her mother to the temple. The vendor packed all the vegetables into gunny sacks and Ila pushed the trolley, with my mother replacing the vegetables, to the temple and back. Ila had to find a solution because my mother was so keen to complete the pilgrimage. My mother's enthusiasm for travel even as she was growing older and weaker resulted in a radio campaign for SBI Life which said, '*Mujhey Ghoomney ka Bahut Shauk Hai*'.

My sister Ila looked for, and found, a solution for my mother.

There is another wonderful commercial which Prasoon made for us, inspired by a story that involves my father. As many parents do, my father used to complain that we were not responsible and were not studying despite having so many conveniences and facilities that his generation did not have. For example, he had to study by the light of the street lamp. I said it must have been very crowded under the street lamp. 'Why do you say that?' he asked. 'It's because everyone's father says that,' I replied.

This incident found its way into a commercial that I did for *Sakshi*, one of the leading newspapers in Andhra Pradesh. The TVC features a father who is unable to shave as he has broken his arm. His son, about twenty-five or thirty years old has come to the village from the city to see his father, and they're talking as the son is giving a shave to his father. The father is talking about how times have changed, and the mother interrupts to tell her son about how far his father had to walk to school, how he had to trudge up a hill and, finally, how he had to study under the street lamp.

That's when the son says, 'It must have been very crowded under the lamp.' The father asks why, to which the son replies, 'Everyone's father says so.'

A childhood memory found its way into a commercial for Sakshi.

Here's where the commercial moves away from my childhood memory. 'I am planning to shift from the city back to this village,' the son says. The father is aghast. 'Are you mad? You are going to do farming?' 'No,' the son replies. 'I'm planning to build and run a school that will have so many lamps that no father will lie to his children about studying under the light of the street lamp.'

One part of the story is inspired by my childhood. The other part, perhaps less apparent to you, is inspired by old age—my father's old age.

Childhood is not the only source for discovering purity; old age is another.

Notice how grandparents get along beautifully with their grandchildren, becoming 'pure' all over again? Neither the grandchildren nor the grandparents are constrained by 'rules', by norms, by practices. They go with the flow, doing whatever makes them laugh, whatever entertains them, whatever they feel is right.

By the age of six or seven, children lose that purity, as society and norms force them to 'behave' and conform, and do the 'right thing'. From this age on, we spend our schooldays, college years and working lives conscious of these pressures. Once we retire, we are free of these constraints, free to become children again, free to become pure. As pure as my uncle, the late H.N. Pandey, became post-retirement. He had his first glass of beer (indeed, of any alcohol) at the age of eighty-five because he couldn't care less. In addition to his late introduction to beer, he splurged on a subscription to *National Geographic* magazine. In his pre-retirement years, he would have thought of this expense as an indulgence, perhaps even as a waste of money. Post-retirement, he couldn't care less.

Thanks to *Nat Geo*, he was so informed on so many issues that he became a constant partner to my brother Prasoon in conversations related to three areas of common interest: films, architecture and town planning.

He once asked Prasoon how film footage, such as songs from Bollywood movies (which is shot at twenty-four frames per second) could be seen on TV (which runs at twenty-five frames per second). Prasoon knew, but his younger colleagues did not. My uncle explained to them that this was done through a process called telecine. Prasoon's colleagues obviously knew about and used telecine, but till then, they had thought that it had to do only with colour correction and not with converting the twenty-four frames per second to twenty-five.

My uncle had the same curiosity and inquisitiveness as that of a child. As long as he was working, this facet was far from visible. Post-retirement, he questioned everything, and sought all the answers! And he had the most amazing answers. Once he cornered Prasoon's close friend Chandu who was a textile designer from NID (National Institute of Design). He was staying at my house on a visit to Bombay when my uncle asked him, 'When you apply mehndi (henna) on your hands or feet, the mehndi is green-brown in colour. When you wash the mehndi off, the patterns that are left behind are red or maroon. If I applied mehndi on a wall and then washed off the mehndi, why doesn't it have the same effect?"

Chandu had no clue, and my uncle explained, 'Human skin has amino acids to which the mehndi reacts and forms a new colour. The walls do not. It's as simple as that.'

When you're stuck, search for gold wherever young and old people are.

That's how simple young children and old people are. When you're stuck, search for gold wherever young and old people are.

*

For centuries, yoga has kept millions of people fit. It continues to do so even today. I have an interpretation of the breathing exercise called Pranayam. It is extremely useful for anyone with a creative bent of mind. In this exercise, you shut one nostril and slowly inhale from the other. You hold your breath for a while. Then shut this nostril and slowly exhale from the other. To my mind, what happens is this—when you inhale, you breathe in the present. When you hold your breath, the oxygen goes to your head and interacts with all that is stored in your brain for years. So, when you exhale, it is a mix of today's learnings and the rich experience of the past.

A great meeting place for the young and the old are the classic Disney animation films. These classics are created by great storytellers who are able to delight the senses of people of all ages around the world. I never miss a chance to see these films again and again. The greatest opportunity came to my brother and me in the 1990s when we were commissioned by Disney to adapt *Aladdin* and *The Lion King* in Hindi, as I mentioned in an earlier chapter. It was the toughest assignment we have ever undertaken in our lives. You can't do anything about the lip-sync which is done to English. You can't touch the music, which is recorded, and it's not just about writing in Hindi, you have to make things culturally relevant for India. It was tough, but we have never had more fun. We had to be ourselves while writing for grown-up Simba, we had to become children while writing for baby Simba, and we had to be like our father for Mufasa the wise king. My suggestion is, when in need of inspiration, go see a Disney classic.

19

Udna Aata Hai? Do You Know How to Fly?

The title of this chapter is my take on the famous saying, 'Feet on the ground, head in the sky'. Anyone who knows how to fly has to know about the ground realities first. Only then can you take off, fly and land in glory.

I have talked about many brands and clients who have done that. Now let me share the stories of two more who have written aviation history in advertising. I am proud to say that Ogilvy is on board as they fly.

The first one is the story of Asian Paints, a company built from the ground up for decades. Asian Paints moved from only corporate advertising in 1982 to both corporate and consumer advertising, addressing various Indian festivals to the widest range of shades—'*Mera Walla Cream*'. The corporate and shades story ran in tandem till the late nineties.

The paint is an expression of pride over the house.

It was in the early 2000s that Ogilvy's Thought Leader, Madhukar Sabnavis, and his team, along with the Asian Paints marketing team, came to me with a new insight. They said that the focus of the consumer is on pride in their house, and paint is only an expression of that. This ground reality gave me the licence to fly when I wrote, '*Har ghar kuch kehta hai*' (Every home has something to say). I still remember having written that emotional piece on my pad—one shot, no change of word or punctuation. I read it to myself and cried. I called up the clients, K.B.S. Anand and Amit Singhal, and said, 'Drop everything you are doing and come straight to my office.' They arrived within an hour. I read out that piece. And this time all three of us cried. We knew we were about to take a flight together.

For the first time, Asian Paints didn't talk about paints or shades. It just took the high ground of emotional pride that everyone takes in his home. India loved it. Its people gave us the commercial pilot's licence!

Today, Asian Paints is not just about paints. It has risen to being the guide for home decor.

Next, look at the journey that the client and Ogilvy have shared as the company changed from Hutchinson Max to Orange to Hutch and, finally, to Vodafone. During this entire process of almost two decades, not a single piece of communication has been pretested before we received a go-ahead. Not one. I think we gave ourselves a commercial pilot's licence from day one.

Big ideas come from the belief that you can fly; big ideas cannot come when you are shackled by research, when you are shackled by conventional belief, when you are shackled by the success of the past.

Big ideas come from the belief that you can fly; big ideas cannot come when you are shackled by research, when you are shackled by conventional belief, when you are shackled by the success of the past. So, when you are not shackled, when you have made the decision to fly, you don't need any strings attached to the ground. And the biggest example of the benefits of being unshackled and of the belief in flying is in the work Ogilvy created for Vodafone when the Zoozoos were conceptualized.

In 2003, we were basking in the glory of the huge success of the Vodafone pug and the little boy, and that was a danger. That is a perfect example of being shackled by the success of the past. Whatever your profession, whatever the business, an extraordinary success cannot be the end of your ambitions. You have to cast it aside and target something bigger, better, more profitable, more impactful.

Zoozoo was a magical concept. The magic happened because the team believed in magic.

That was the challenge for the Ogilvy team working on Vodafone as we strategized on IPL-II in South Africa. This was an era when consumer habits were changing, and holding on to their attention was an increasingly difficult proposition. The tournament spanned a continuous period of forty-odd days, with two matches being played on some days. How long before the consumer, a big cricket fan, tires of virtually any piece of communication if he sees it time and again? It would be more than fatigue; the ad might actually begin to antagonize the consumer.

As we pondered on the problem, Hephzibah Pathak, then heading team Vodafone in Ogilvy, suggested a preposterous notion: a new ad for every single day of the tournament. If knowing how to fly is a qualification, Vodafone, to me, has always been a company of squadron leaders and air chief marshals, right from Asim Ghosh, Sandeep Das, Harit Nagpal, Kavita Nair and, more recently, Martin Pieters. The first to react to Hephzibah's idea were Harit and Kavita. Amazingly, they, too, believed that it was a great thought.

As consensus was reached on Hephzibah's suggestion of forty-four ads, the scale of the thought began to sink in, and Rajiv Rao, heading the creative team on Vodafone, must have died a hundred deaths as he contemplated the task being discussed.

We were discussing a strategy where we needed Rajiv's team to come up with forty-four ads for Vodafone. These forty-four ads needed to be connected to each other. And each of them needed to be refreshing, entertaining and impactful.

As the meeting broke up, the only thing we knew was that forty-four commercials had to be made. We had no clue of what the commercials would be about, who would produce them and how they would be made.

Rajiv went to the drawing board and returned with an, umm, something. It wasn't a human being, it wasn't an animal, it was just a 'thing'.

Rajiv's team wrote a few scripts featuring this thing (it didn't have a name, then) and the thing's family and friends. Rajiv drew prolifically, and intense meetings resulted in more and more scripts.

The trouble was, as everyone fell in love with the thing and the scripts, there were a few problems. Big problems. The only way to convert the ideas into reality was to use animation—and animation would be too time-consuming and too expensive.

But Rajiv pressed on, not shackled by either past success or current knowledge. He was committed to seeing this campaign come to life and decided to reach out for solutions, immediately flying to Bangalore to meet his most trusted and valuable sounding board, Prakash Varma from Nirvana Films.

Rajiv and his partner, the late V. Mahesh, had worked with Prakash on Vodafone earlier, notably on the pug campaign, so there was an ease in the relationship and an extraordinary amount of trust in each other, not to speak of mutual respect.

They began with these 'givens'.

The films had to be made.

Animation was both too time-consuming and too expensive, so animation, the most obvious solution, was no solution at all.

The time available was finite and non-negotiable.

Prakash worked backwards from the 'givens'. If the characters were not to be animated and if the characters were neither humans nor animals, the only solution was for humans to be put into these 'thing' costumes. His solution was to work in South Africa with some technicians whom he knew. He proposed a cost and a timeline, and that worked for Vodafone.

The only problem was that Varma was suggesting something that had never been done before, and everyone fears the unknown.

Not Vodafone, though. They made a huge leap of faith, backing Rajiv's confidence, having worked with him many times earlier.

So, the Vodafone team, Rajiv's team and Varma's team, all went to South Africa. The costumes were designed and tried on. To ensure that the 'things' stay small, Varma's team furiously hunted for petite women who would fit into the costumes. They began shooting for the first set of approved scripts and were racing against time, with the first match of the tournament a few days away. They had all but finished the first four films, which would air on day one of the tournament, and uploaded these edits to Bombay for the senior management at Vodafone to see and approve.

Rajiv met me at my hotel as soon as I had checked in, and we went immediately to the studio. It was early in the morning, but the place was a beehive of activity, with tens of sleep-deprived technicians and editors fighting against time. At this point, not a single person other than those who were working in the studio had seen the final cuts. I saw them and was stunned, and I said this was the most brilliant piece of communication that I had seen in my life.

Later, I learnt that the entire studio was waiting, petrified, for my reaction. The tension ended when they heard yelps of laughter emanating from the viewing rooms, and, as the laughter continued, they knew that they had a winner.

We stepped out for a cigarette as the enormity of the films began to sink in. Someone offered to bring me some coffee (it was 10.30 in the morning), and I rejected the notion and asked them to bring in some beers. I replayed the films in my head and wondered, why couldn't I have ever thought of something as brilliant as this?

Zoozoo was a magical concept. The magic happened because Rajiv, Prakash, Vodafone and their teams all believed in magic. 'Experts' marvelled at the perfection in the animation and wondered how it was done; we used to laugh, as reviewers referred to the great animation. If I had not known how the films were shot, I would have been another 'expert' trying to figure out how the campaign was done.

The rest is history.

History was made because the entire team simply refused to work with what seemed to be limitations that would shackle them. They refused to stay in the charted territories, choosing to find magic in unknown and unchartered territories. They looked at the 'givens' as just those, 'givens'. Anything else, including making real shooting look like animation, was not a 'given'.

History was made because all those involved had the balls to try the untried. They had balls; very big balls.

Too often, we forget that the path more trodden doesn't lead to anything new. Everyone has used it; everyone knows where it ends and what it looks like. Use this path, and you will find yourself bang in the middle of everyone else.

Rajiv and Mahesh, when they created the Vodafone pug, chose the road less travelled. Once this road was discovered, many others followed. Faced with a new challenge, Rajiv, once more, chose the less travelled road.

Whether in advertising or in any other business, it is the sky less flown that promises exciting possibilities. Ask Vodafone. Ask Asian Paints.

20

Payback Time

If you are in advertising, it's unlikely that you will become a Tata, Birla, Ambani or a Bill Gates, all of whom, apart from their belief in philanthropy, also have resources to fund projects for social good. But don't feel deprived, because God and your own learning have given you some important weapons—the power of imagination, the power of your pen and the power to communicate effectively. It is no mean wealth. Use it and see the world around you change.

Over the years, I have grabbed every opportunity with both hands since 1986 or 1987. Suresh Mullick gave me the chance to write the lyrics of his national integration film. I was able to write '*Mile sur mera tumhara*'. The film became the most loved piece of social communication, and the song almost became the second national anthem. The kind of response I got was such that it motivated me to do more work in the non-commercial space. All of a sudden, my mother started believing that I was doing something more meaningful than selling soap. The most beautiful and touching words were: 'I wish your father was alive to see this work. He would have gone to all his friends and said, "So now you know what my son does."'

'Mile sur mera tumhara': *My mother started believing that I was doing something more meaningful than selling soap.*

A few years later, Roda Mehta, Gerson da Cunha and some others convinced the Government of India and the Department of Education that the National Literacy Mission campaign should be created by a professional agency. Ogilvy got the mandate. And I got the opportunity to do something of national importance. The campaign, '*Chalo Padhayen, Kuch Kar Dikhayen*' (Let's Teach and Do Something Meaningful), became a national hit. During this time, I worked closely with a phenomenal human being, Mr A.K. Bir, who was both a renowned cameraman and a director. This two-in-one role saved money, which we had very little of. Mr Bir was also not doing this for money. With one hand tied behind our backs, Mr Bir, I and Meera Kalia, a young copywriter, looked for creative ways to make a great campaign. We got friends from theatre, my nieces (Swati and Shruti), to act, among others. We begged Unilever and got a song for free. And we made many films that ran for years. In return, all of us got the blessings of a nation and satisfaction that no awards can give. In fact, we got the awards too, including the David Ogilvy Award for best Social Service Campaign from Asia Pacific. I still have a certificate signed by David himself.

Such was the response to this campaign that one day, we got a call from the human resources ministry asking us to remove the offer of free teaching booklets from the commercial, as they could not cater to the number of people who were offering to teach. I remember telling them that why not take the commercial off the air, as I was not interested in moving people emotionally and then not delivering. I don't think I would have said that to a commercial client in those days. Such is the depth of emotion when your public-service work gets traction.

Ogilvy had done great work for the Cancer Society of India in the eighties. Our commitment to this cause was very much there before I met Mr Y.K. Sapru of Cancer Patients Aid Association (CPAA). At that point of time, I had already lost a sister to cancer. When Mr Sapru asked me to help wherever possible, I said, 'Whenever you say.' We knew there was no money to spend; there was only money to be obtained for the association from donors.

Around this time, my long-term partner, Sonal Dabral (by now posted in Ogilvy Malaysia), shared an idea with me. The idea was simple. An old man in a bus gives his seat to a teenager who has lit up a cigarette. The voice-over says, 'Be nice to smokers, they don't have much time left.' This was a very powerful idea for youngsters who don't believe in stories of death, as they think they are too young to die and cancer happens only to old people.

Remember, we had no money. So, I spoke to Prasoon, who agreed to do it gratis. I spoke to my good friends, Mahesh Mathai and Srila Chatterjee, of Highlight Films. They said, 'This is a great idea, we'll produce it for free.' We made the film which turned out to be a masterpiece. Then I showed it to MTV and other major channels, all of whom said, 'We are on, we are running it.'

How can a line like 'be nice to smokers' not grab your attention?

It was a great piece of work which we later entered for various awards. Then one day, I got a call from my Asia Pacific chairman, Miles Young, who said, 'Send me a media plan for this, a proof of release of this ad, because it's going to win the Best of Best at Asia Pacific, but they suspect it's a scam.' I was livid, but then I sent him a ten-page media plan from eight channels that ran the campaign, and the rest is history.

The moral of the story is when you do pro bono work, give your all to do a great job, from the conception of the idea to the execution and through to the release. Don't worry about accusations or suspicions. Put your hand on your heart and you will get the answer.

I, along with Rajiv Rao, went on to do the 'Dead Horse' ad for CPAA, which later won India's first Double Gold at Cannes, Double Grand Prix at London International, and just about everything else. Above all, the free media coverage that CPAA got worldwide cannot be measured in monetary terms. As Mr Sapru opened the champagnes for team Ogilvy, some jealous voices in the industry were questioning the ad's authenticity. All I said was, 'They can sit on my horse!'

When you do pro bono work, give your all and do a great job.

A number of teams have worked for CPAA since then, have created great work and continue to do so. Our client Pidilite has been supporting CPAA for years. And we contribute with our ideas to all these events.

We had a great cause and the most credible celebrity—now we needed a great idea.

This chapter would be incomplete without the polio story. It was at the turn of the century that Ogilvy was selected by UNICEF and the Ministry of Health for the polio immunization programme. Amitabh Bachchan had agreed to do the campaign pro bono. We had a great cause and the most credible celebrity. What we needed was a good idea. Not the run-of-the-mill, government-type endorsements. I got one idea and I rushed to Mr Bachchan and said, 'Sir, everyone calls you the symbol of the Angry Young Man, because of your roles in your earlier super-hit films. How about you playing the Angry Old Man in this campaign?' He loved the idea, and I and Ajay Gahlaut wrote the scripts. Mr Bachchan helped fine-tune them. When I presented the script, the clients fell off their chairs, particularly the bureaucrats. 'How can Mr Bachchan shout at people?' I replied, 'Of course, he can and should. He is going to do it like a dad who is upset with his child. There is love behind the anger.' There was a young man from UNICEF who got it the first time. He helped. Then we played our trump card: Mr Bachchan said it would be impactful. That was it.

For the next few years, we worked with director Santosh Sivan producing multiple ads. The fieldworkers, UNICEF and the ministry people did exceptional work. And then, after years, on 12 February 2014, India was declared polio-free! Can any award in the world give you that kind of joy?

My personal satisfaction with these kinds of campaigns is such that at Ogilvy, we have asked all groups to take up a cause of their choice and work on it as an ongoing commitment. So, while I drive Jaipur Foot (prosthetics [read about them on http://jaipurfoot.org/]), CPAA, BMC (Bombay Municipal Corporation), WWF (World Wide Fund for Nature), sanitation, energy conservation, etc., there are teams that are committed to the Mumbai Police, the 'Cleft to Smile' campaign, adoption, the Head Injury Foundation, Childline, Akansha, CRY (Child Rights and You), and many more.

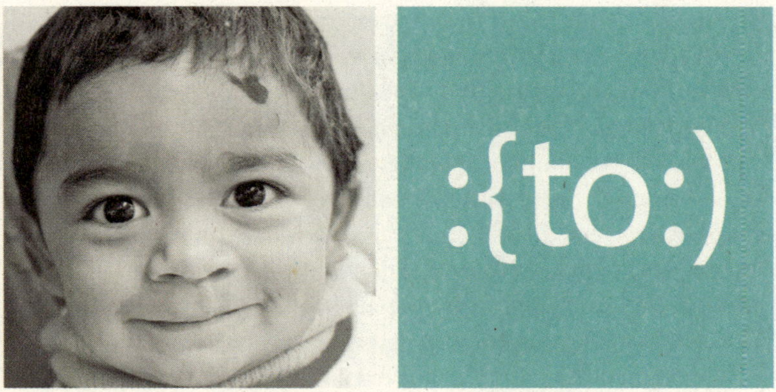

We look for causes that we commit to for the long term.

Scam Ads

I have talked about my love for the railways and the Indian Postal Service, as a child. Today, I am a happy man that my commercial for the Indian Railways ran at the Commonwealth Games in Delhi in 2012. Three thousand volunteers enacted the commercial at the closing ceremony. The Indian Postal Service signage that we see all across the country is designed by Ogilvy—something that I offered to do gratis, and it worked!

This book is written from the heart and this chapter is particularly close to my heart. If I do not say what I feel, I would be cheating myself. So, here is something for the next generation.

Don't worry about accusations or suspicions. Put your hand on your heart and you will get the answer.

You have two options. Do scam ads for barber shops, dentists, weight-loss clinics, your girlfriend's boutique; or pick up an issue and do path-breaking work on it. It's possible. Start with something small in your colony. If it brings about a change, and even wins an award, good for you. Probably, if the idea is good, it will spread to the city, then the state, followed by the country. If it's really great, shoot it on video, and put it on the Net. It will spread like wildfire and may win you an award. A poster for a sweet shop will do nothing of the kind. Even an award is difficult because the world and the juries have got smarter.

Now, I am going to make a few suggestions. I am fully aware that my 'well-wishers' will say, 'Hey, he is pushing the government's agenda because he worked on their political campaign.' Hold your horses, and think, for a change. I did not work on anyone's political campaign when I did '*Mile sur mera tumhara*', or conceived campaigns for the Indian Postal Service and the Indian Railways. I worked for India and its agenda. So, what should be on our agenda today?

- Women's Safety
- Swachch Bharat
- Girl Child Education

- Sanitation; and
- Energy Conservation

Pick up one where it matches the agenda of someone who has the infrastructure and ability to give meaning to your idea. My message to you is: *each one, choose one*. You may not win a statue, but probably someday someone will make one of you.

21

Failure Isn't Really a Bad Thing

Failures can happen any time in life, but if one is lucky, the failures confront you early on.

A significant lesson that I learnt from a failure was that life was a journey and not the destination. Every milestone is nothing but an indicator that you are on the right track; there are many other milestones to be reached and passed.

Like many other things in my life, this lesson, too, came from cricket.

I was a fairly decent cricketer, having captained the St. Stephen's College and then the Delhi University team that went on to win the all-India Rohinton Baria trophy. Other cricketers playing the same tournament included Kapil Dev, Arun Lal, Dilip Vengsarkar, Sandeep Patil and Roger Binny. Cricket-wise, things were going fantastically for me. I was named captain of the Rajasthan Under-22 team for the C.K. Nayudu Trophy, and the big names that I've mentioned just now also made their debuts for their respective states in what was the inaugural year of this competition. Almost as a matter of course, each one of us played for our states in the Ranji Trophy.

Kapil Dev and the others named, who were obviously more talented than I was, were also hungrier and more hard-working. They took the Ranji Trophy selection as an opportunity to excel, get noticed and reach the next level of the game. Not surprisingly, all of them ended up playing for India. And then there were others who were not blessed with as much talent as these names, yet made it to the India team, thanks to their sheer dedication and hard work.

For me, the story was different. I was so satisfied and overwhelmed by the idea of playing alongside great players in the Rajasthan Ranji side, such as Hanumant Singh, Salim Durani, Parthasarthi Sharma and Kailash Gattani that I completely mistook my selection in the Ranji Trophy team as a great achievement and a destination, rather than as an important milestone.

Instead of working hard like the others, and perform, compete and excel at this new level, I focused on getting the flannels tailored for myself—so that I could look the part of a great player. Needless to say, I failed and did not make it to the next level of cricket. My cricket journey ended there.

Today, I treat every day as a session at the nets.

Fortunately, I was able to recognize this mistake quickly and early. So, always keeping my disastrous cricket experience in mind, henceforth I never looked at any opportunity or achievement as something that I could take for granted.

As a trainee account executive, I worked hard to be one of the best. When promoted to the position of account executive, I took a fresh guard to play this new role, telling myself that I am starting to bat on zero. The same continued during the rest of my journey in advertising. Every day was a new day, and every opportunity a fresh start.

I still smart from the way I misread the opportunity that came my way in cricket and I refuse to make the same mistake again. Today, I treat every day as a session at the nets. I look at work we have done and try and figure out how we could have done it better. I review campaigns that did not make as much of an impact, and attempt to assess where we were wanting.

Even on occasions when we are invited to take part in a multi-agency pitch for a new account and my team tells me that the so-called pitch is just a formality and that the account would be awarded to agency X in a decision already made, my advice to them is simple. I tell them that we must ensure that we pull out all the stops and present some great work, if only to make the client regret that he is not working with us, and give him sleepless nights. The bonus would be that such an exercise would challenge the team mentally.

I look at my career in the context of milestones, not destinations. When we win an account, I do not stop to celebrate, but look ahead for the next account. I do the same with great campaigns or awards and recognitions. All of them are milestones to me.

After thirty-three years of being in this business, I still get up every morning hoping to write the best ad of my life.

No, I don't want to be just a Ranji Trophy player in the world of advertising. I want to play Test cricket and compete, and outperform the best.

There are other cricket-like lessons that I've learnt. Like the time when I believed I deserved a promotion and didn't get one. I complained bitterly to Suresh Mullick. I had performed well, I felt. I had outperformed many others, I felt. And yet I wasn't promoted.

It was Suresh who calmed me down with a cricket analogy. 'You're playing well and your runs will not go unnoticed,' Suresh said. He reminded me that the selectors were watching and they had an eye on me. Thanks to Suresh, I remained calm and patient, waiting for the selectors to choose me. They did.

*

Recently, there has been much talk about footballers in the UK being spoilt by not having to do their internship. Till as late as a decade ago, the youngest players in a team had the onerous responsibility of carrying the kitbags of the seniors, cleaning their muddied boots, and so on. So it was with cricket for the twelfth man and the others not named in the playing XI. These were all apprentice-like positions and opportunities.

There are many lessons from my failures for young graduates from distinguished institutions. When these bright young men and women take up their first jobs, they need to forget some of the chapters taught to them in the last year of their curriculum—how to be a CEO, how to be a chief architect, how to be a head designer, and so on.

A job is not learnt from the textbook alone; it is learnt on the job as well. In advertising, you have to carry artworks, write presentations, and run various errands in your first job, irrespective of the repute of the college that you went to. In marketing, you have to report to the senior salesman as his or her assistant, and travel to the smallest of markets around the country. I do not know if this practice still exists, but in my younger days, all fresh marketing executives of Hindustan Lever had to spend eight weeks in a village called Etah in Uttar Pradesh in the home of a rural consumer to understand their needs, behaviour, consumption habits and aspirations. These lower-middle-class homes were very different from the urban homes that the new recruits came from; they just had bare essentials and were devoid of most comforts.

Those who took this rural stint in their stride came out on top, becoming the Vindi Bangas, Harish Manwanis, Nitin Paranjpes and Sanjiv Mehtas, while many others not only assumed leadership of Hindustan Lever, but also of many other multinationals around the world.

They had chosen to forget the chapter in the management school about being a CEO, but they practised every other chapter one after another till they went on to become one.

Just look back at the early days of Sachin Tendulkar and Rahul Dravid. There was cricket and more cricket, runs and more runs. They moved on from one tournament to another, continuing to work hard or even harder. The sunglasses came much later.

4

OGILVY & ME

22

David Ogilvy and OMW: Horses for Courses

Running a company with a global network is much like managing the Centre–state relationship in Indian politics (the company being the state). There are national matters where power rests with the Centre and then there are those where the state is supreme. The only advantage with a global company is that unlike national politics, the states and the Centre are always run by the same party. Yet, this requires great understanding of each other's needs, mutual respect, tolerance and patience for it to be a win-win situation. If you are positive and confident, there is a lot to learn from global minds so as to add to your knowledge pool about your own country or region. During my career, I have met a lot of great minds from the Ogilvy network. Let me talk about a few of them.

I was very fortunate that a couple of months after I joined Ogilvy, Benson & Mather in August 1982, Ad Asia, a premier event for the advertising industry, took place in India, and David Ogilvy made his first visit to the country. I hadn't read much about advertising, but obviously I had read about David Ogilvy before I joined Ogilvy.

David Ogilvy was a legend. The more I read about him and heard about him, the greater the admiration that I had for him. And here I was, a few months into this new job, getting an opportunity to meet him. Many years later, I would meet him again, not as a virtual fresher, but as a responsible and valued part of his global team. In 1982, I was too young and too junior to get any time with David. My interaction with him should have been limited to an introduction and a nod, but thanks to the fact that I was a smoker, I got to see a little more of him. David had recently 'given up' smoking, which meant that he didn't carry cigarettes. On both occasions that we met, he kept looking for me and bummed cigarettes off me (which hurt my pocket as I was earning just Rs 2000 a month); this allowed me to have far more conversations than would otherwise have happened.

I feel I was fortunate that I was in India. If I were part of Ogilvy anywhere else in the world, I might have had nothing to do with David. In 1973, David had retired as chairman of Ogilvy & Mather, and had moved to Touffou in France, where he had an estate; he was no longer involved in the agency's day-to-day operations. However, David came out of retirement just before I joined, to serve as Chairman of Ogilvy, Benson & Mather in India.

Ogilvy was then not a part of WPP; 51 per cent of it was owned by the Indian management. David believed greatly in the India opportunity and the Indian management (he has said many times that India is his favourite country), putting great faith in Mani Ayer, whom he considered his personal friend. David also had a lot of respect for Suresh Mullick. The India team's connection with David was through the relationships that Mani and Suresh had with David—and as both Mani and Suresh would end up mentoring me, I learnt so much about David's philosophy and beliefs through them, absorbing all that they said about him. David sold the company to Martin Sorrell's WPP in 1989, and in these years, I had little direct interaction with him barring the two meetings in 1982 and in 1986, as I was too junior; my interaction with my international partners began in earnest with Shelly Lazarus. But we'll come to the incredible Shelly later.

Let's first get to Martin Sorrell. People would like to believe that Martin is a control freak—nothing could be further from the truth. Martin's name is misused by his managers in the operating

With David Ogilvy's wife Herta at Cannes—with an image of David in the background.

companies so as to help them achieve their own ends. Martin would not even be aware of many of the things that his managers claim that he has an opinion on. His interest is in communication, in the health of his companies, in the finances, in corporate-governance issues, in the stock price and in WPP's shareholders. Martin does not interfere in the running of the companies and has little interest in decisions that ought to be taken by his local managers—which is perhaps why WPP does so well globally. The fact that India is so important to WPP now, and yet the Indian operations are run totally by Indian managers underlines his belief that global businesses are best run by managers who know the lay of the land.

If cigarettes helped me spend more time with David than was warranted by my designation, it was cricket that helped build my relationship with Martin. Martin is a huge cricket fan, following the game from wherever he may be in the world. In London, he watches matches at Lord's whenever he gets the opportunity. He plays as well, taking part in charity matches for causes that he believes in.

Planning for one of his earlier trips to India, he mentioned to Ranjan Kapur that he wanted to play a cricket match in India. He asked him to get me to sort it out (he was aware that I had played first-class cricket). He wanted the teams to be formed from employees of the three larger agencies WPP had in India those days: Hindustan Thompson Associates (HTA); Contract (which was considered a separate company, though it was 100 per cent owned by HTA); and O&M. Martin also wanted a couple of former India cricketers to play so as to add some flavour to the match.

I did the maths and decided that each of the three agencies would contribute six players, making it eighteen players. Martin would make it nineteen. That would leave us three players short. I requested Bapu Nadkarni, Eknath Solkar and Ashok Mankad to play, and they all agreed.

We now had twenty-two players, and the next challenge was the composition of the two teams. I had some thoughts on that. I wrote to the managers of HTA and Contract asking each of them to send me the names of their six players—and their heights. They wrote back and asked me why I wanted to know about their heights. I told them that it was for the cricket whites that we needed to play in.

Martin was to captain one team, while I would captain the other. I divided the remaining twenty players into two teams.

Martin came to the ground and discovered that his team was called Short Legs XI and that mine was Long Legs XI. I had created the teams based on the heights of the players. Martin came up to me and said, 'You cheeky bastard.'

For me, Martin is a human being and no more.

That match set the tone for my relationship with Martin. It allowed us to be relaxed, frank, trusting and honest with each other—and that makes for a profitable working relationship.

During another of Martin's visit, I planned something else. When you entered the office, from far you could see a poster outside my room with 'WPP' written on it. WPP did not have an office at Ogilvy. So when Martin came, he saw the signage and walked to my room. From close, you could see the small letters between WPP. It said, 'Worldwide Office of Piyush Pandey'. 'Cheeky bastard' is what he said to me again, as he laughed.

'Cheeky bastard' is a phrase that Martin loves to use, and I've been described as one by Martin on more than two occasions. In 2000, I was flying to judge the Clio Awards at Aspen, Colorado. The perks of being a juror meant that I flew first class on British Airways. First class was a rarity as WPP's policy did not allow it. I was in the first-class lounge in London, waiting for my connecting flight to the US, when I bumped into Martin. I walked up to him and said, 'Hi, Martin, Clio is paying for this trip. Just in case you call up Rane (my colleague and then Finance Head of Ogilvy in India) and ask him who is paying for this.' 'You cheeky bastard, did I ask you?' He said. 'No, you didn't, but you would have called up Rane; I just saved you a couple of pounds on the phone call,' I replied.

When we meet now, conversations are relaxed and direct. Martin discusses larger issues with me, such as the company's reputation and corporate governance, two areas where he spends considerable time and energy. We hardly ever talk about work or revenues. Indeed, sometimes we have to contrive devices which get him to look at recent work that has been done; I do not think that he has ever asked for a formal review.

I've learnt so much from Martin—perhaps because I saw him as a human being and no more. Approach Martin with fear or trepidation or guile, as many do, and what you have achieved is to ensure that Martin doesn't relax. That's your loss.

If I gained by my relationship with Martin, the other notable relationship that helped create the Ogilvy that we see today is my relationship with Neil French. Neil, too, to my advantage, was a great fan of cricket, which helped immensely in finding an immediate connect. Cricket made us great friends, and allowed me to talk to him with ease.

When Neil came to India for the first time, his reputation as a creative legend preceded him. His work flirted with the edge, winning awards and accolades; our big work in India, those days, was for Fevicol, Cadbury and Asian Paints. Little of the India work was flamboyant, even if they more than delivered on the briefs and resulted in client delight.

I requested Neil to energize and motivate our creative team, and make them hungrier. However, I underlined that I did not want comments on Fevicol or Cadbury or Asian Paints. I explained that we created advertising that was loved by consumers, while he did work that disturbed consumers and created waves in the creative world. I underlined that the existence and success of the India company lay in creating work that connected with people, not with juries on awards shows.

Neil respected this and agreed. While I did not want disruption or criticism of the kind of work that we did in India, I was more than happy if he addressed issues such as complacency and innovative thinking. Neil did just that, leaving the India team charged, motivated and rejuvenated.

To understand the stark difference between our cultures and viewpoints, Neil disliked the Vodafone pug commercial—he thought it was too soft and sweet. Neil liked being naughty in his work; we, in India, liked being nice. And consumers in India, over the years, have made it clear that they like 'nice'.

There's another aspect of Neil's reputation that precedes him—the reputation of him being a bully, and naughty and nasty. When one spends time with Neil, as I have been fortunate to, one gets exposed to the softer, gentle, caring side of him. He had a great relationship with my mother who wasn't fluent in English. Neil would call my mother each year on her birthday and sing 'Happy Birthday' to her, followed by a long conversation. He did this every single year.

This, by the nasty, bullying Neil French! There is a nicer side to everybody; there are many dimensions to every human being. My relationship with Neil taught me that—to look for a dimension to a human being other than the one that is obvious or most talked about.

We make the mistake of defining the people we meet as sharply as possible. Black or white. But look for the grey. Both Neil and I could have dismissed each other on the basis of our opposing views on the 'naughty/nice' issue; it was in our persevering with the relationship that we got to see aspects of each other beyond these narrow confines. It's then we learn that there is a beautiful aspect to every individual— '*kuch khaas hai hum sabhi mein*'. The trick is to look for it.

We make the mistake of defining the people we meet as sharply as possible. Black or white. But look for the grey.

From Neil, in whom I had to discover the beautiful aspect, we go to Shelly Lazarus, whose beauty is immediate and apparent. I have huge admiration, respect, love and affection for Shelly. Shelly brings great enthusiasm, exuberance and energy to everything she does, and it's no surprise that she's been named the Most Powerful Woman, the Most Influential Woman, the Most Influential Person, and so on by many big publications, industry bodies and organizations. Shelly has been a believer in the David Ogilvy school of thought, fully imbibing and practising it. As a result, she was not a great believer in awards, even in the Cannes Lions, preferring to believe in work that works. When I first met her, she had never been to Cannes.

It was when I was appointed the Chairman of Cannes Film Print & Poster Juries, she decided to make her first visit to Cannes, where she mentioned that her trip was solely because of me.

Shelly ran a huge company, and one would imagine that there would be both praise and criticism when people speak of her, but

I have never met anyone who has had anything negative to say about Shelly. Shelly exudes love, and therefore attracts love.

Over the years, my wife Nita and I have become very good friends of Shelly and her husband, George. They've visited our house in Goa and we have spent some memorable times together. Each time I am in New York, I make it a point to let Shelly know, and Shelly, George and I have a wonderful meal together.

Shelly Lazarus is a woman who is 100 per cent *khaas*.

Miles Young and Tham Khai Meng (C)*: Partners at the global level.*

When Shelly was the global head, Miles Young was the regional head, and therefore someone that I had a great deal of interaction with. Ogilvy India first diluted from 51 per cent to 40 per cent and eventually became a fully owned WPP company. Miles was in the region during the management transition in India, when Ranjan Kapur was on his extension. Miles kept insisting that I take over from Ranjan. He said that the move would be a natural one, and something that was anticipated by colleagues in India as well as outside. I was tentative, concerned that managing the business would come in the way of the focus on the creative product. Miles kept the pressure on from 2000, even as I kept refusing the role. He didn't let up. In the second half of 2003, when we were at an offsite office in Hong Kong, he said that he was not going to wait any longer. He called twenty colleagues to where we were and said, 'Cheers, here is our new India chairman!' The elevation to chairmanship further increased the intensity of our relationship, as by now, Ogilvy India was clearly a jewel in the crown of Ogilvy & Mather Worldwide. Miles surprises all with his knowledge and understanding of India, but it is his understanding of the business and administration, as well as his people-management skills that I'm astounded by—and I learn a lot from him. There was a fear among my colleagues in client servicing when I was named chairman. While, by now, I was confident of my capabilities as a creative head, running an organization as large as Ogilvy was now needed skills that I thought I didn't have. Miles had run the Asia Pacific region with success and aplomb for thirteen years, when he was named as Worldwide CEO of Ogilvy. With all his rich experience in Asia and Europe, some people gave him little chance to succeed in the US. But Miles is a determined and audacious man. Not only did he take this challenge head-on, he also appointed his creative partner from Asia Pacific, Tham Khai Meng, as the worldwide creative director.

These two men were on a mission quite similar to the one Ranjan and I had been on earlier, albeit at a global level. They wanted to see Ogilvy as a creative powerhouse. They went about it hand in hand against all odds. It is their grit and determination, commitment and belief that ensured that the Ogilvy network won the Network of the Year at Cannes for four consecutive years, from 2012 to 2015.

So, how did this transformation in creative reputation happen? Did we throw out our global systems and processes? What happened to our financial system? Did they become less important?

While the creative output is paramount, it is the systems, processes and general management which allow the creative teams to excel. And these cannot be flouted.

If you've decided to play the game, then you play within the rules of the game. Yes, you circumvent some rules from time to time—otherwise you would be a bureaucrat—but you have to have an agreed plan which is the basis of all that you do. The financial plan is what makes the difference between a gamble and an investment. If your plan says that you are going to earn 100 rupees this year and, therefore, you need to invest twenty rupees, it becomes easy for somebody to say okay, go ahead and do it.

The men in black. As we became a creative powerhouse, we built our reputation.

If you don't have a plan, then the decision is like punting—and large organizations cannot be punters all the time. You can punt here and there from time to time, but you can't be a company of punters, and that is where having a plan, having a system, is extremely important. I actually feel empowered that I can take this risk because I know there is a system to protect me. I can do the trapeze because I know there is a safety net. I may fall and make a fool of myself, but I will not die. Many people believe that I do not follow or respect systems and procedures, but that is as far from the truth as one could imagine. Am I driven by the system? No, I will never be driven by the system. I am empowered by a system, which is why I have a great amount of respect for it. So, all of us have to follow certain rules and all of us have the liberty of breaking certain rules, as long as we are playing a game which is not dangerous to individuals, to clients or to the health of the organization.

If you've decided to play the game, then you play within the rules of the game. Yes, you circumvent some rules from time to time—otherwise you would be a bureaucrat—but you have to have an agreed plan which is the basis of all that you do.

Many younger colleagues in advertising complain about excessive management, saying that their freedom is being curtailed. To them my advice is, understand the systems as I have done, and, when you feel that you are being stifled, discuss this with your seniors. Try and imagine that the systems are a safety net, not handcuffs. The systems are there to allow you to perform, not to kill your creativity.

I may sometimes disagree with some policies, but do I want to play in a well-managed team? Of course, yes.

23

Leaders Emerge: Ranjan and Rane

I don't think you can train anyone to be a leader or a CEO; CEOs are born CEOs. The CEO brings with him (or her) his own thinking, his own outlook, his own vision, his own way of looking at life. If being a CEO is all about ticking boxes, you are virtually saying that anyone could be a CEO. Imagine being told, if you tick boxes A, B, C, D, E and F, the job of the CEO is yours.

If I had to tick boxes, I would never have become the CEO of Ogilvy, let alone the chairman. Look at Kunal, who we have just promoted to CEO, and how different he is from me. There is no way that he and I could ever tick the same boxes.

To me, a fantastic CEO says, 'I don't tick A, B, C, D, E and F, but I tick L, M, N, O, P and Q.'

There are traits that any manager needs; one is hygiene. That would mean ticking five to six boxes. These would include looking after the health of the company, looking after its people, looking after its administration, and so on.

But where is the inspiration? A CEO has to inspire. A CEO needs to think differently as well as confidently communicate and execute his vision and his inspiration. He should and will make his own boxes.

If all this could be defined on paper, every goddamned person would be a CEO. So could all those trainers who write bestselling books like *How to Win Friends and Influence People*. If you ask me, whoever buys books to become a CEO is a fool. To say, when you meet someone, say these seven things, and he will become a friend has to be goddamned nonsense.

You don't tell people that if they want to run, they must first remind themselves that they have to breathe. Breathing comes naturally to all. A lot of knowledge comes naturally to you. And then what you bring to the party is your own wisdom, your own ambition, your own aspiration, your own dream, your own experiences, your own judgement. I don't think you can formulate that. That's why I don't believe in overtraining.

That's the problem that I have with the B-schools in the country; students are not taught how to be themselves. They're told that they are future CEOs and they view everything from that viewpoint. Imagine a twenty-three-year old, walking into Ogilvy with an attitude that says, 'I'll run this show soon.' He comes crashing down to earth in his first few days, as someone, just a few years older, would tell him to take an artwork to a client.

Like I've said before, when in doubt, I go back to cricket. Imagine if the selectors sent out a memo that said, here's a checklist for those who want to become the captain of India. Then we would have coaching classes that ensure that the students ticked all the boxes; all of them would be captain material. Of course, in theory. In practice, they might all be good. But one will emerge as the leader, because that one demonstrates a vision, a dream, a plan.

*

Ranjan

In 1994, when Ranjan Kapur returned to India as managing director, Ogilvy & Mather was still number three or four in terms of size. In creative terms, we were beginning to make a change. Ranjan understood the potential and formed an unusual triumvirate, a triumvirate where he was the captain and S.N. Rane and I were his partners. He declared, 'We will be India's best and biggest agency on the back of great creative work.' Thereon, between Ranjan and Rane, they looked after all that was needed to be done to run a company successfully—client servicing, planning, financial, administrative, HR, compliances, and so on, allowing me to lead the creative challenge.

With Ranjan Kapur, the man who created the successful triumvirate.

Most importantly, Ranjan took care of the relationships at the top—with our regional office, the head office and with Martin Sorrell. If you work in a network agency, or indeed a multinational firm for a reasonable length of time, especially in a globalizing world, you would have seen periodic eruptions of stress and conflict with the head offices. Ranjan took care of those that erupted during his tenure.

In the early 2000s, I did a public service ad which won significant international acclaim and almost every prestigious award that one could name.

The ad was seen as objectionable by a brand that we had nothing to do with—or so we thought. In this complex world of commerce, and mergers and acquisitions, a multinational company that we did work for had been bought over by the multinational company that had found the ad objectionable.

The drama was played out at the head offices and there was immediate pressure for India to withdraw the ad. Ranjan ensured that none of the pressure was felt by my team and me—and refused to withdraw the ad. He even sent a cartoon showing his head on a platter which he offered if the powers that be insisted that the ad be withdrawn.

A lot of knowledge comes naturally to you. And then what you bring to the party is your own wisdom, your own ambition, your own aspiration, your own dream, your own experiences, your own judgement.

The ad wasn't withdrawn; Ranjan's head remained with him—and my respect for Ranjan and all that his team did went up many, many notches.

That's how companies succeed and prosper—by strong team work. It took a Ranjan by my side that allowed the creative teams to have the confidence to push the edges, to experiment with new ideas, to delight our clients and audiences alike.

This incident, in many ways, changed the way Ogilvy India thought. It gave us fresh momentum and energy, and an extraordinary sense of freedom. Knowing that we had Ranjan looking after our backs, we could go on and be at our creative best.

Ranjan demonstrated what leadership was all about: in times of crisis, stand up for the team and take the brunt of the heat, allowing the company to function normally and with confidence.

Many years later, I was caught in a scenario precisely like the one I mentioned, and with the memory of what Ranjan had done etched vividly in my mind, I did the same: defended the team and the work staunchly. We had created an ad that was not intended to be insensitive, but ended up offending some quarters. As Ranjan did a decade earlier, I explained to my international counterparts the context in which this ad was created, the way Indians and India saw the ad, and refused to budge.

Thankfully, my colleagues understood and accepted my point of view.

What Ranjan did in defending the controversial work in the early 2000s has become the DNA of the agency. A decade later, I did the same as he had done. A decade from now, if a similar situation arises, someone will do the same as Ranjan and I had done.

*

Rane

Rane is a genius at both finance and administration. Outside of Ogilvy and the WPP system, he is barely known, as he consciously stays away from the limelight. Rane's story is fantastic because, though he joined Ogilvy as a finance professional, over a period of time he grew to love advertising. A self-motivated, tremendously hard-working individual, Rane has quietly contributed to all the achievements of Ogilvy India. It is because he does his job so efficiently that the rest of the team can focus on the product and on client delight.

Rane became not just the CFO but also the COO of the company, having joined as the number two in the finance department. After joining Ogilvy, he studied company affairs and law, equipping himself with the tools needed to run a company. However, for a finance person to succeed in the communications business, he or she needs to understand the nuances, quirks and idiosyncrasies of the business. In time, Rane learnt to understand what makes good communication, by talking to my team and me about the work that we created. Rane takes great delight when ads are well received by critics and consumers, and celebrates award wins like any other creative person.

His dictum has been simple: you do good work and the money will come easily, and when that happens I will manage the money well.

Now, post-Ranjan, Rane and I have worked together for over ten years. When Ranjan left, we had to reconstruct the team. What Ranjan had created was a body, which was Ranjan and his two arms—Rane and I. Without Ranjan, I had to take on all the external responsibilities that he would shoulder, while Rane took over the entire internal load.

Rane anticipates developments that cannot be anticipated.

By now, I was named chairman, but over a period of time, it was apparent that Rane was equally responsible for the running of the company, which led to him being named co-chairman.

Anyone who has worked in Ogilvy India will tell you how relaxed all of us are about the financial management of the company. Rane's preparedness seems to anticipate even those developments that cannot be anticipated. When the world was affected by the Lehman Brothers crash, we hardly felt a ripple in Ogilvy India.

Rane has been a fantastic support to Ogilvy India in general and to me in particular. Having Rane around has been like doing the trapeze at the circus with the knowledge that nothing can happen to you or to all those taking part in the act, because we have the world's best safety net to protect us should anything go wrong. Rane has been the safety net for Ogilvy India.

In hindsight, there is a lesson I must share. If you're what we loosely call a 'creative person', or in any business that creates, involve your money man in the passion of the journey that the company is undertaking. The more he understands and appreciates the magic of the business, the greater his ability to help the business grow.

Ophelia Gomes

I have to talk of someone who has become an integral part of my life Anyone who has known me for a reasonable length of time knows that, to put it mildly, I am technologically challenged. However, you would also know that when you send me an email, I acknowledge the mail almost immediately (if it comes to me in reasonable office hours) and reply in detail in a day or two. Similarly, if I am invited to an event, I always respond to the request for an RSVP. If I confirm that I will attend an event, I do. Joining all these dots, you would think that this does not sound like someone who is technologically challenged and that I am perhaps harnessing all the power that is available in my smartphone.

That's far from the truth. I have a system that is far stronger and more reliable than any digital system you are aware of. The 'system' is my assistant, Ophelia Gomes.

Ophelia manages my email. She reads the mails, prints them out, sorts them into her understanding of priorities and brings them to me. I dictate replies to her and she answers the mails for me. She manages my diary and ensures that I do not double-book myself. On my part, I *never* make a commitment without checking with Ophelia. And it's not just the correspondence and the appointments that Ophelia looks after. She probably knows more about my personal finances than I do, considering she handles all my bank correspondence as well.

Anyone who has worked with me at Ogilvy will tell you that I am able to survive because of Ophelia. She's been my colleague for over twenty years now. She's a godsend assistant, completely dedicated to her job. As I grew in Ogilvy, so did the need for administrative discipline and compliance. Ophelia ensures that all my internal paperwork, form filling, claims, and so on are made well in time—never ever late. There are some incredible lessons to be learnt from Ophelia. The first is her passion and dedication to her work. She is at the office each morning bang on time. She focuses completely on her work, with no time at all for idle chatter or gossip. In the evening, she finishes her work punctually and leaves for the day.

Once Ophelia leaves the office, she is unavailable because that time belongs to her. That's the second learning: she balances her work life and personal life perfectly. If she gives her company 100 per cent commitment during office hours, she gives her home 100 per cent commitment for the rest of the day. I respect the lines she has drawn. I will not call her after office hours, even if some issue seems to require urgent attention. When I stop to think about it, what on earth requires attention post-office hours and cannot wait till the efficient Ophelia is at her desk the next morning? Ophelia has been my partner for the greater part of my career. It's a partnership of understanding and mutual respect.

Having Ophelia as my partner has freed up my time, allowing me to focus on the creative product. She ensures that, even when it comes to issues which would have consumed my time at home, like my personal finances, the time I need to devote is minimal.

Do yourself a favour, whatever it is that you do, find yourself colleagues you can trust and delegate work to. The more you trust and delegate, the more time you have to spend on things that really matter to you.

24

Indian Advertising Has Been Unfair to Its Women

When I first joined Ogilvy in 1982, my first boss was a wonderful lady called Swati Bansali. She was called an account supervisor, but an account supervisor in those days shouldered far more responsibility than an account supervisor does today. She oversaw a team of men and women who swore by her; she had clients who believed in her and trusted her with the task of finding solutions to their communication problems. She was a tough boss at work, and a sensitive friend to all of us once the workday was done. We were mentored and nurtured by her.

We also had the stalwart Roda Mehta, the lady who single-handedly changed the way the media-planning discipline was perceived, bringing the job the positive attention that it deserved. Roda entered the business when she had to evangelize the importance of media planning and buying. Most clients believed that all that the media department did was to buy space in newspapers and magazines. There was very little understanding and appreciation of the environment in which the messaging was received by the consumer. Roda convinced clients that she and her team brought the understanding and finesse that was required for their brands and, consequently, deserved to get paid adequately for this expertise. I've learnt a lot from these women.

Over the years, through most of my career, two CEOs of Ogilvy were women: Charlotte Beers and Shelly Lazarus.

I often wonder why we are not seeing more women heading advertising agencies in India. Not that we haven't had any; we've seen Tara Sinha heading her own agency. And we've seen many, such as Roda Mehta, heading the media business. In media, we've seen many just below the top: Lynn de Souza, Meenakshi Menon, Ketaki Gupte, Sunita Gopalakrishnan, Kalpana Sathe, Jasmin Sorabji, and so on.

We need to ensure that the women stalwarts and stars in our business stay in the business for long enough—something that banks in India have done successfully, with Arundhati Bhattacharya as chairperson of State Bank of India, Chanda Kochhar as MD and CEO of ICICI Bank, Shikha Sharma as MD and CEO of Axis Bank, Naina Lal Kidwai as country head, HSBC, and many others. These ladies are not just running successful financial corporations, but are thought leaders whose opinions are taken into account while drafting national policy.

Why aren't more women heading advertising agencies? It's a failing on our part (and that includes me). We've not been sensitive enough to the needs and compulsions of a woman. A woman is born with many more facets than a man; she is as intelligent and competent and hard-working as any man—but she is also the nurturer of the family. Somewhere, the two roles create a conflict, and she is forced to choose one over the other.

This conflict has to be resolved by the business, not by the woman. We have to look at ways and means to ensure that a woman who takes a break because she has a baby has the desire to come back to the business when a satisfactory support system is found for the child and the rest of the family. I have great admiration for companies that have made recent announcements on paternity leave and extended maternity leave. I believe that such decisions not only enable women stars to contribute to the nation, but will also make for better fathers in the future.

Why aren't more women heading advertising agencies? It's a failing on our part (and that includes me).

We haven't realized or been sensitive to the fact that a huge treasure of knowledge is lost when competent women leave our industry.

Women leaders also bring sensitivity to a business, something that men often lack. Many businesses with few women at the top, such as advertising, become boys' clubs.

At Ogilvy (and other agencies as well), we have a bunch of rock stars who are women in senior positions. We currently have Hephzibah Pathak running the Bombay office (the largest advertising agency office in India), we've had Vibha Desai heading the Delhi office, and Preeta Singh heading the Bangalore office.

We need many more women to join and to rise. But will we be able to retain these women? Will they want to stay back and become chairperson or CEO of Ogilvy or another agency? Times are rapidly changing, and perhaps technology will force change, thanks to the ability to work from home, connect virtually and be connected 24×7 from wherever you are.

We, those at the top of the advertising agencies in India, have to roll the wicket to allow them to score a 300 or a 400!

Throughout this book, you have run into frequent references to my mother and my sisters. I have experienced their talents, their ambitions, their frustrations, their limitations, and I have also seen their success. I would love to see the same happen for many more women, particularly in the field of communication.

25

Domestic Multiculturalism

What applies to global companies operating in multiple countries, also applies to national companies operating from different locations in one country. Successful national companies ensure that there is a knowledge and resource pool that defines the culture, ensuring a high level of output from any location. In addition, there is a locally knowledgeable team that understands local nuances and client expectations.

Many do not realize that there's a lot of great work coming out of Ogilvy offices beyond Bombay and Gurgaon. While the other offices do not have the luxury of a roster of clients who present opportunities for great work, they still manage, every year, to push the envelope on some of the great clients that they have. For example, in the days of Mohan Menon, Madras was a rocking office. The kind of work that came out of Madras was often the envy of the leading creatives in Bombay and Delhi. Take the fantastic TVC that came out of our Madras office for something as uninspiring as the change in name of a brand—when Sakura (manufacturers of film rolls) became Konica.

The Madras office produced an animated TVC, where a man shouts into a cave, 'Sakura'. The voice echoes back; only it doesn't say Sakura, it says 'Konica', the new name for Sakura. What a great piece of work!

Successful national companies ensure that there is a knowledge and resource pool that defines the culture, ensuring high level of output from any location. In addition, there is a locally knowledgeable team that understands local nuances and client expectations.

The Madras office produced, in the early nineties, the first-ever music video for a brand in India, for TI Cycles. None of us in Bombay or Delhi had even considered the property. Madras saw the opportunity, as MTV and Channel [V] had launched, and they took advantage of it. Today, they do great work for Vodafone South.

Whether it was the Konica campaign or the TI Cycles campaign, the common thread that ran across the clients of the Madras office was the depth of the relationships that they had with the agency.

The most extraordinary story of relationships in India is from our Madras office, and features Dollar Company, the firm that made Hadensa, the piles cream.

Dollar was never a very big client, but the promoter, Dorairajan, was a great friend of Mani Ayer's—and for Mani, the size of the revenue did not come in the way of ensuring that the brand got the attention that it deserved from us. Dorairajan was always dressed in a veshti and shirt, an unusual sight in an advertising agency. He was a very demanding client, provoking colleagues to say that he behaved as if he owned the agency.

In 1976, there was a plane crash in which the manager of Ogilvy Madras, Tej Kapur, sadly, was one of the victims. At that time, there was no one senior in the Madras office. When Dorairajan heard of it, he walked into the Madras office, sat down in the manager's seat, called up Mani Ayer (who was in Bombay), and told him, 'You don't worry; I have taken charge.' Till such time as Mani could figure out a solution, our client Dorairajan looked after the office.

There is no greater learning from Madras than the story of Dorairajan. What can be better than clients believing that they are a part of you?

The media in India, especially the trade media, tends to focus on just Bombay and Delhi; so, work from the other offices gets short shrift. If the work from Madras surprises you, look at what our Bangalore office has done. Bangalore houses our youngest metro office. Calcutta, Bombay, Delhi and Madras preceded Bangalore. Our first manager at Bangalore, R. Sridhar, did not just establish the office, but made a significant contribution to Ogilvy's reputation in India.

There are many indicators to the contribution of the Bangalore office. The first is the fact that, thanks to Sridhar and his passion and belief in direct marketing, Ogilvy Direct was born in Bangalore—the beginning of the agency's understanding and confidence in one-on-one communication.

The second measure is the outstanding work done on some brands that the Bangalore office has handled over the years. Brooke Bond came to us when their operations shifted from Calcutta to Bangalore. Titan was launched by this office, and continues to be a client till today. The office has done some great work for 3M's Post-it, a mountain of remarkable Titan work, the campaign on Allen Solly, and on ITC's snack brand, 'Bingo!'. The list of great brands and great work is endless; I would need a few pages just to list them.

The most important measure of the contribution of the Bangalore office, however, is on the people front. Some outstanding talent has been discovered in this office, and it has been important enough for us to send our best people to work there. I'll list some names so that you get a sense of the extraordinary resources that the Bangalore office has seen. Google the names and you will discover what each one is doing now—heading creative agencies, heading media agencies, playing national roles in the agency business as well as on the client side. As I list them, I'm astonished as well.

Chintamani Rao, Sanjay Nayak, Preeta Singh, Harish Vasudevan, Ramesh Ramanathan, R. Gowthaman, Prateek Srivastava, Devraj

Tripathy—all of them have had significant stints in our Bangalore office.

Brooke Bond came to us when their operations shifted from Calcutta to Bangalore.

When the Bangalore office wanted more creative resources, we moved Rajiv Rao and the late V. Mahesh to Bangalore—despite the fact that the two were critical to the Vodafone (then Hutch) business. Thankfully, we had a fantastic and understanding client who allowed us to move the central creative process from Bombay to Bangalore. Could we have given the Vodafone responsibility to a new team? Of course, we could have, but both the agency and the client understood the unbridled passion that Rajiv and Mahesh had for the brand. We decided that as long as the brand was well looked after, we would, unusually for this business, have

Vodafone handled out of an office which was in a city where the client wasn't even present!

There are more instances of inter-office osmosis. Malvika Mehra went to Bangalore, and with Amit Akali, created the magical work on Bingo! And then, there is the truly outstanding contribution that our relationship with IBM made to the agency. The IBM account hastened our understanding of working with multiple offices in multiple locations worldwide, handling international projects, and later, playing a role in the creation of what was then called the Lenovo Hub, which addressed the communication needs of Lenovo for the entire world. Today, my colleague Poran Malani continues to attract international assignments to Bangalore.

I should have started this chapter with the Calcutta office; after all, it is where Ogilvy was born in India. It's where Mani Ayer worked, where Suresh Mullick, my mentor, worked.

Ogilvy was born in India when Calcutta was a significant centre of commerce and many of India's largest companies had their head offices here. The foundation that was laid by Mani and Suresh remains strong—so, even as Calcutta's influence on commerce has waned, the output from there on national brands such as Cadbury, Asian Paints and Vodafone that require communication based on local insights enhances the agency reputation. Even now, Ogilvy Calcutta is named Calcutta's Agency of the Year quite regularly.

The very fact that clients felt the need for communication based on truly local insights and nuances, based on our experience with the Calcutta office, encouraged us to launch Dakshin, the agency that specializes in understanding consumer aspirations in the four southern states. However much most of us know about communication and creativity in general, we often find ourselves woefully lacking in understanding the culture and nuances of discrete markets, and hence the need for offices across the country. We overlay the local understanding, which, for example, the Calcutta office has, with creative talent that, by and large, understands the region. So, Sumanto Chattopadhyay is responsible for the Calcutta office as well, in addition to his responsibilities in

Bombay. By placing some wonderful people and making Sumanto take charge of the Calcutta office, we recognized the fact that Piyush Pandey doesn't know the local nuances of Bengal and the east as well as Sumanto and his team do.

When Vodafone needed a heightened understanding of Andhra Pradesh and needed work in Telugu, we opened an office in Hyderabad. The Vodafone account was the bread and butter of the Hyderabad office, but the jam was in being able to win new business there. The work on Vodafone and our reputation nationally helped us with the *Sakshi* (newspaper) account and the Deccan Chargers business.

If one looks back at the career paths of many of the seniormost people in Ogilvy nationally, or at the career paths of many talented individuals who have left Ogilvy to build their careers elsewhere, you will find that many had one of their first jobs in an office other than Bombay. As a result, if we transfer someone from Bombay or Delhi to a smaller office, the transfer is seen as both recognition and an opportunity.

Imagine a year when all five Ogilvy offices in India fire at the same time with equal ferocity and energy. We've often had two offices simultaneously firing on all cylinders; less often, we've had three offices in tandem. I wait for the day we have all the five on top of their game simultaneously. The only way that will happen is if we continue doing what we have done: encourage and excite the finest talent we have into moving to cities other than Delhi and Bombay.

What is the lesson here? If you become bigger, you will have more offices. But don't let go of your culture, no matter how small the office.

26

Who Is the Man of the Match?

When creating work in an agency, it's difficult to pinpoint who precisely contributed to the work. Some of the contributions are obvious, like the individual who wrote the first draft of the first script. Obviously, he or she deserves credit. After that it becomes hazy. Contributions may come from those directly and explicitly invited to comment on the original idea, but, as is often the case, contributions can come from those in the agency or the ecosystem who hear about the idea and make their suggestions.

The challenge arises when one lists those who contributed to the piece of work. If the work goes on to be popular with the consumer or with critics or ends up winning awards, each of the names on the credits list enjoys an incredible upside. There is a downside to it as well.

If you liberally distribute credit, it can give young people a false sense of ownership, which leads to a false sense of confidence. Just the name on the list of contributors to an award-winning piece of work can do that. That's why one has to be careful in crediting anyone for a piece of work. The same is true for marketers. I've seen a number of marketers genuinely believing that they are better than they are; the fact that the work they have approved is recognized at awards shows often makes them more vocal in their views on creatives.

Just being on the credits list leads youngsters to say to themselves, 'I have arrived.' Winning an award is not a destination; it is just another milestone in a long journey. The day after the award is won, it's back to the drawing board with your thinking cap on, working on the next brief to sell products or services for the clients that you handle. It is the danger of the downside that has led me to remove names from the credits list, apportioning all contribution to Team Ogilvy.

My conviction that this is the right thing to do stems from all those who contribute to the success of the work but find no mention in the list of credits. For example, where would any of us be without the boy who brings us tea from the canteen or rustles up steaming hot coffee just when you need it? Where does he find mention in the credits? What is the role that the spot boys played in the award-winning TVC? Where are they mentioned? What about the junior sound engineers or the junior editors, slogging away through the night just to ensure that the commercial is perfect? Where do they find mention in the credits? Always think of the office boy, the spot boy, the junior sound engineer and the junior-most editor.

To many of us, the idea of giving someone credit, when he or she might not quite deserve it, comes from a false sense of generosity. And this generosity might end up doing significant damage to the individual who is the beneficiary of the act, and might do great harm to him and to the company he works for.

Winning an award is not a destination; it is just another milestone in a long journey.

Over the years, I have learnt to read the fine line between deserved credit and 'generous', not-quite-deserved credit. As I continue to make the distinction, I realize that this view, again, comes from cricket. The man of the match is not a solitary hero; the winnings are shared by the team. It is always the team that wins or loses, not the individual. Similarly, it is the agency and the client brand that wins, not the individuals in the agency or the client who were obviously involved in the creation of the work.

*

Anyone in any business that is in the media spotlight must think about the balance between rewards and awards. Rewards are important to everybody in any walk of life, in any profession, at every strata of society. Whatever it is that you do, you want a return for the activity, for your contribution. You want a good career in return. You want a good life for your family.

But when you are in a business that receives media attention and there's media involvement, like the film business, theatre, music or advertising, rewards are only part of the story.

Awards get into the picture. Not just in the 'creative' industries that I mention above, but into almost any industry vertical. In addition to monetary rewards, be it the salary and bonus on the personal front, or the profits on a corporate level, awards become important.

Everyone needs some kind of a pat on the back from peers and experts in the vertical because these awards are seen as unbiased substantiation of a success story or an achievement.

Much as awards in advertising are both hyped and contentious, the corporate world, too, takes great pride in being recognized. Walk into a CEO's office and you're sure to see statuettes, figurines, certificates and photographs pertaining to awards that the CEO is proud of having received, often on behalf of his company.

Simply put, awards are a form of recognition. The greater the credibility of the body behind the award, the greater the pride the recipient feels. This holds true even if the award carries no cash or monetary component.

There is no better example than the awards that are bestowed on members of the armed forces. Every award is celebrated and the awardees are respected, celebrated and honoured. How can one not admire the recipient of the Param Vir Chakra, awarded in acknowledgement of 'the highest degree of valour or self-sacrifice in the presence of the enemy'?

It is the approach to awards that is extremely important. No member of the armed forces destroys an enemy area or kills members of the enemy forces in search of an award—even if it is the very act of killing the enemy or destroying enemy property that sees him being considered for an award.

That should be the approach to awards in the creative world as well; that when you did something, you did it for a purpose that was clearly defined as a part of your job or responsibility, and your performance is seen by some as exceptional and they choose to present you an award.

Unfortunately, in advertising, we often see that award chasing becomes the objective of many professionals.

An award for the purpose of an award is self-defeating. Over the years, I've seen many who have won some national or international award early in their careers—and disappear thereafter.

These awardees may forever have (and treasure) the physical statuette or whatever, but they miss out on the pride in their body of work and the real recognition. The award became the purpose, rather than creating communication that addressed the brief and was loved by the consumer.

To me, the greatest award is when a barber tells me, 'Sir, I saw your Fevicol ad,' or a man on the street tells me, 'I love *Chal Meri Luna,*' or some client tells me, 'I saw that new Asian Paints TVC, it's wonderful.' For me, there is no greater award than that.

If any of these pieces of work also wins an award, it's a bonus.

Do I love getting awards? Of course, I do. I'm like any other normal human being. Who doesn't love recognition? But what I enjoy more than an award is the ultimate recognition—when consumers love the work I've done.

Let me share a few stories that are, to me, more gratifying than the awards at Cannes.

The first was at Ad Asia in Jaipur in 2003, when I was staying at Rambagh Palace. I was waiting for my car at the portico when the security guard, about seventy years old, sporting a magnificent moustache (about a hundred times better than mine) and outfitted in typical Rajasthani attire with a fabulous colourful *safa* on his head, said to me, 'Sir, when did you leave Jaipur?' I said that I had never left Jaipur, and that I worked in Bombay, and keep returning 'home' whenever I could. The gentleman laughed out loud and said, 'So, you are bonded to Jaipur like Fevicol?'

I don't think I could have got a better award than that in my life. Here's a man on the street, who obviously is a consumer of news media, who knows that I work on the Fevicol account, and who creates a joke that recognizes my work on the brand. What I learnt is this: not only has he seen and been entertained by the Fevicol ads, he wants to share an 'idea' that he has for Fevicol.

Could his joke of my being 'bonded' to Jaipur find its way into a Fevicol ad in the future? I don't know.

Thousands of people have written to me over the years, saying, 'I have a Fevicol idea,' 'I have a Cadbury idea,' and so on. Each time I receive such a letter or mail, I feel that the writers think they 'know' the brand as well as we do and have been impacted enough by the ads to want to create communication for the brand.

What could be a greater recognition or award than the consumer loving your work?

When you start chasing awards is when you forget what you have been hired for. You have been hired to sell somebody's message. When I say message, it might be a public-service message, it could be the government's message, or it could be for services or products.

You're selling a message that needs to reach and affect a defined set of people. In your greed for an award, you forget the original target audience. Your new target audience becomes a jury at an awards show, jurors whose expectations you think you know and whose expectations you attempt to meet. By doing this, you've completely lost track of the original target audience, and the message that you would now create will not appeal to them, the only people who matter to the brand that you work for.

I received my greatest 'reward' just a few months ago at Dabolim Airport in Goa. I reached the airport to take a flight to

Bombay when I discovered that I'd left my wallet at my residence, which meant that I did not have identification of any kind.

Without any ID, there was no way I could enter the airport. My house is forty-five minutes away from the airport, so there was no way to go back, pick up the wallet and return in time to catch the flight. I immediately asked my driver to wait, and, hoping against hope, I walked up to the security staff and explained my predicament, showing him the printout of my ticket. He looked at me like I was unhinged, and explained patiently that I needed a valid ID, without which he could do nothing.

As I resigned myself to missing the flight and to the trek back home, an employee from the Marriott Hotel in Goa (a guest relations executive who normally goes to receive important guests) walked up to the security guy and said, 'Listen, this is Mr Piyush Pandey, don't you know him? He creates fabulous ads like Cadbury and Fevicol, and so on.' The security guy stared at me, smiled in recognition and waved me into the airport.

Neither the Marriott employee nor the security guy presented me an award. What they both presented me with is a memory that I will cherish all my life and recognition for my work that is greater than any award any jury could ever give me.

Do not chase awards; chase good work.

I would urge young people who have won international awards to ask themselves one question. Did your mother, uncle or close friend understand the piece of work that won you an international award? If you had to explain the ad, it means that the ad was created for the award, not for the consumer—then you've lost the plot.

If you win an award for work on a Lifebuoy or on a Tanishq or on a Titan or on a Cadbury, on work that the world has seen and understood, your mother, rather than being foxed, is likely to say, 'I knew it was going to win. I loved it so much.'

There's one more measure: if you won an award for a client, has the client stayed with you? Has the client's business grown?

Ogilvy has won more awards than anybody else in India in the past twenty years, but awards matter little to clients if their businesses haven't grown.

I remember how, in 1983, Ogilvy had won the campaign of the year award for an Asian Paints campaign, and we were very close to being fired by the same client despite having been awarded for work on the account. As far as Asian Paints was concerned, the award-winning campaign hadn't worked. Asian Paints believed, and correctly so, that the work that we were doing for them was not Indian enough, that the work was failing to move the consumer.

How did it matter how many awards the work won, if the paint was lying unsold in the warehouses?

Awards have never been responsible for Ogilvy winning new businesses. What has got us new accounts is our work. I've received calls from CEOs saying that they want Ogilvy to work on communication because they love the work on Fevicol or Asian Paints or Vodafone or Tata Sky or Titan or Bajaj Pulsar . . . There's hardly any mention of awards. What these CEOs see is the correlation between the health of companies and their advertising.

Do not chase awards; chase good work. When you do win an award for work that consumers enjoy, celebrate the moment, celebrate the recognition.

27

BJP Campaign: The Walk to the Capital

It's so easy to forget history. When we look at the composition of the current Lok Sabha, with the BJP (Bharatiya Janata Party) occupying 288 seats, we forget that the victory wasn't as simple as it looks.

In July 2013, an opinion poll conducted by CNN-IBN indicated a divided India. The BJP was ahead, but only just. It seemed certain that the country was headed for a hung Parliament, with most of the opinion polls showing that no single party would win a majority and would have to cobble together a coalition government with other parties.

On 7 September 2013, the BJP declared that Narendra Modi, the then chief minister of Gujarat, would be its prime ministerial candidate. This was a master stroke, even as the media was speculating on whether or not the BJP would name a candidate for prime minister in case a BJP-led coalition was voted to power. The BJP's announcement of Narendra Modi as its prime ministerial candidate suggested that he would be the prime minister of a BJP government, not a BJP-led coalition government.

Shortly after, came the audacious target that the BJP set for itself and announced: 272+ seats. In other words, a simple majority without the help or support of any other party.

Who would the BJP choose as their communication partner? After numerous presentations, the BJP awarded the account to Soho Square, a WPP agency that Ogilvy managed. The first task for Soho Square was to understand the subtle shifts in voter sentiment.

Once we got an understanding of what the voters felt, we had to come up with what the voters wanted to hear and what they would believe.

The brief was crystal clear: There would be only one name, Narendra Modi, in all communication, which led, unambiguously, to '*Ab ki baar, Modi Sarkar*'.

There were a hundred possible ways to take this thought forward, while ensuring that the messages resonated with the voter sentiment which we had identified. For print and for outdoor, we kept it simple, riding on the back of rhymes styled after the *doha*, '*Bahut hui gundagardi, lootmaar, ab ki baar Modi Sarkar*,' for example. (There's been a lot of crime and robbery, it's time for Modi's government.)

For the TVCs, we decided on using the voice of the people. Real people and their real voices and their real frustrations and concerns. When I presented the first film campaign which used real people, capturing testimonials of their views and pains, the seasoned politician was stunned. What's this? Just one human being shot against a black background? Wouldn't that be boring? We insisted that it would be far from boring; that it would be riveting. We told them that the starkness would make the films real and believable.

I showed them how this might look, using the Amitabh Bachchan Cadbury work that we had done to address the worms issue, as an example of how this campaign would eventually look. We argued that we needed to see the fear, the tiredness, the anger, the anguish, the hopelessness clearly.

There would be only one name, Narendra Modi, in all communication.

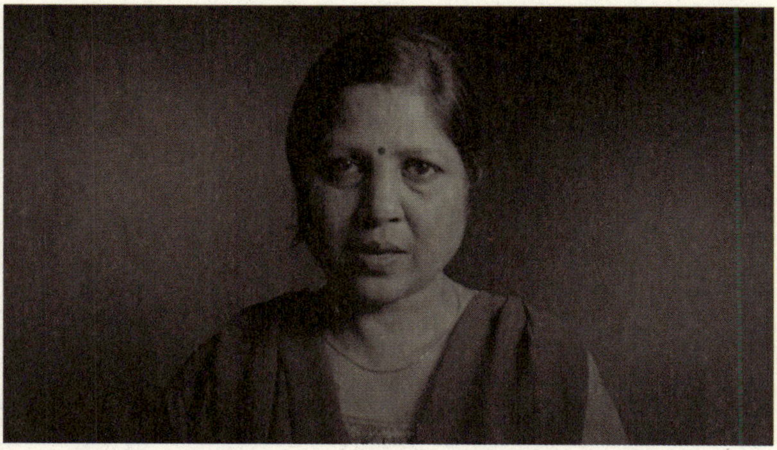

Finally, we ended up doing an astonishing eighty of these testimonials.

It was a tough campaign to buy, and a tough one to sell as well. The BJP team talked it over quickly and gave us the go-ahead.

We explained that we would work with real people; we could not have a Piyush Pandey talking in both Hindi and Tamil. Finally, we ended up doing an astonishing eighty of these testimonials. We took real people, real stories, real issues. The raw material came from the BJP briefing team. For each state, they knew the issues that mattered, they knew what pained the constituents the most. The BJP workers had been working on this for so long that they had everything pat and ready for us, which is why we could roll the films out at the speed that we did.

The other big factor in the success was the clarity in the role of definition. Our job was, simply, to create the communication. We didn't have to worry about media or social media or placement or planning; that was someone else's headache. This freed us to concentrate on the task at hand.

Simple communication reaches and touches many more people

We were brought on board in February, just before the T20 World Cup. We wanted to ride on its extraordinary popularity and viewership, but the 'testimonial' campaign would not work when the audience wanted to watch cricket. There was no way that a sad story would find acceptance.

I explained to the BJP think tank that we needed a new, radically different campaign that spoke to this younger, less involved audience. I presented an animation campaign after a lot of selling. (To the best of my information, I do not think a satirical political campaign in animation has ever been done, so I couldn't show them any references.) Moreover, I shared my idea of cricket-specific ads without *any* politician in the campaign. They weren't convinced. We were—so we brought in an NID-trained animator, and created four films as a proof of concept. When they saw the films, they loved them instantly, and we ended up doing many films in the campaign.

The whole exercise was fantastic because of the mutual trust and the ability to work as a seamless team. The sheer volume of output in those three months is testimony to the mutual trust and respect. In less than seventy-five days, we had created over 200 commercials, 150 radio spots, and over 1000 print and outdoor creatives in every major language in India. And that the BJP won is a bonus for all who worked on the account.

We needed a new campaign that spoke to the younger, less involved audience.

One of the most beautiful things about the entire campaign was its simple language. By and large, political-party language, particularly in Hindi, is pretty heavy. The words are not what people speak. They are correct by the book, but ridiculously difficult.

All lines in this campaign were from peoplespeak—'*Ab ki bar Modi Sarkar*' was as simple as the brief. '*Janta maaf nahin karegi*' (People will not forgive) is something on the lines of what we have said or heard so many times since childhood: '*Bhagwan maaf nahin karega*' (God will not forgive you). Or for that matter, '*Acche din aane waale hain*' (Good days are around the corner). Have we not consoled friends in grief or trouble, saying, 'Don't worry, acche din aane wala hai'? Don't all these little phrases remind you of '*Chal Meri Luna*', '*Thodi si pet puja, kabhi bhi, kahin bhi*', '*Chutki mein chipkaye*', or many such simple lines? They do. Simple communication reaches and touches many more people—and we saw that in this campaign. Remember, every little line that you have ever spoken or heard as a child is a line that may be worth its weight in gold when you work on your next campaign.

5

ADVERTISING TODAY AND TOMORROW

28

The Indian Advertising Business

On the surface of it, the Indian advertising business looks like it's booming and healthy. That's only on the surface. Dig deeper and you see a different picture—a picture of a business that needs fresh thinking, reinvention and investments. These changes are needed not just in the agencies, but in the marketing companies as well.

The most important area where we need to see reinvention is in the people who work in the business. Advertising needs to excite young people with different abilities and talents to be part of the industry, and it needs those over forty to be shaken up, because the business and the needs of the business are changing. Simply put, we neither have the talent that we sorely need nor are we able to attract those that have the talent.

Consider this: India's ad expenditure is much lower than a country like Indonesia's, let alone China's. Today, we talk about an economy that could grow at over 8 per cent. If the ad expenditure grows a few percentage points above the GDP growth (which is a reasonable assumption), we are talking about a business that is poised to grow at 11–12 per cent.

Where is the talent that can deal with this pace of change?

India's prime minister, Narendra Modi, has emphasized the need for skill development and enhancement if India is to grow to the potential we see before us. Similarly, advertising needs skill development and skill enhancement to meet the challenges of the rapidly changing world.

Advertising needs to excite young people with different abilities and talents to be part of the industry, and it needs those over forty to be shaken up, because the business and the needs of the business are changing.

Advertising agencies need to look at the changes in the environment and figure out what is required to win, as the rules of the game are changing. The worry is that few in the business in India are analysing the situation and contemplating the need to try something new.

When in doubt, the answer, to me, is always available in cricket.

Pinch-hitter

Where was this term in use in the limited overs tournaments in 1975, 1979, 1983 and 1987? Nowhere.

We first heard of the term when Sri Lanka decided that, to have a chance of excelling in a game that was changing, the only hope was to take a look at the game afresh. To reinvent the way the game was played.

The year was 1992. All through the World Cup, Sanath Jayasuriya and Romesh Kaluwitharana made the purists stare in awe as they opened the Sri Lankan innings, playing the game in a way none had done before. Abandoning the conventional approach of 'seeing off' the new ball and being satisfied with a sedate 40 for no loss after 15 overs, the two went hammer and tongs at the pacers, leaving the opposition stunned as they struggled to set a field to this unconventional strategy.

The gamble paid off, and four years later, Sri Lanka, having changed the rules of the game, won the World Cup for the first time, in 1996.

It was only Sri Lanka that saw the opportunities that the changing game presented even as the others couldn't or refused to do so. The old game had been dead and needed a new lease of life.

There is a lesson to learn from what Sri Lanka did in 1992. So, look at how the 'game' has changed in communication, and get into a position where you can win in the near future.

As a business, we need to discuss and understand what the new demands are and how best to meet these challenges—and we need to do this in conjunction with our clients.

If the pinch-hitter concept was an experiment, we need to experiment as well. It's nothing new, actually, and it has been done before. Earlier, we believed that the current structure of the business was poorly poised to deal with the imminent opportunities that rural India presented. We discussed the issue with our client, Unilever, and proposed that we experiment together in this area. Our experiment involved hiring and training villagers to communicate brand messages. Within months, we had trained as many as 15,000 villagers to promote Unilever products in rural India. Unilever instantly agreed and actively supported our efforts in the search for efficient solutions to market in rural India.

It was our own unearthing of a pinch-hitter.

In this fast-changing world of advertising, we need many more experiments, and many more clients to partner with in these experiments. In our early forays into the rural experiment, both Unilever and Ogilvy made significant investments in an area that both believed would be valuable and lucrative in the near future. However, while the opportunities lay in the future, we had to identify talented individuals who would be inspired and challenged by the opportunity, and train and groom them for the responsibility.

We had to identify, invest in and back the Kaluwitharanas of this new game in advertising.

It was relatively easy for Unilever and Ogilvy because we were both committed to a long-term relationship with each other. We were invested in each other; the success of one half of the team automatically meant success for the other half.

That's an important illustration of how advertising in India needs to change. We need to stop looking at only short-term gains and short-term targets, and invest in each other for the more distant future. It's this investment that makes the relationship stronger and richer.

For advertising agencies, the more mature you are in making investments in client relationships, the greater the chance that the account will remain with you.

Yet, as we look around us, we see agencies win and lose large and lucrative accounts because they do not resource the accounts adequately. Forget the future, the accounts are under-resourced to deal with the present.

When we invest in a strong team, the relationship begins seeing all goals and challenges as mutual goals and challenges. It underlines that the relationship is collaborative and that we look at a shared future.

What would happen if we under-resourced, say, the Vodafone account or the Unilever one or Cadbury?

The clients will look for other communication partners for one or other parts of the business that we currently handle—because their business imperatives would force them to. We'll see competitors chipping away at our business, or whittling them down to smaller and smaller accounts. Once we lose little bits of the business, our ability to handle the core will be questioned—and we will, in a matter of time, lose the business altogether. All because we refused to see the long term, didn't invest in adequate resources, and refused to experiment in a changing world.

Equally importantly, clients need to make adequate investments in their communication partners. If the client fails to compensate adequately, the agency will be constrained to provide services or service quality that is justified by the income. In a competitive environment, under-compensating the agency could result in a direct competitor gaining a share of the voice and the market by way of a more visionary view on communication.

We have seventy-five to eighty members in Team Vodafone, headed by two of the most talented and well-paid resources in

Ogilvy India: Hephzibah Pathak and Rajiv Rao. It is the strength and quality of the team that gives Vodafone comfort and confidence in Ogilvy. It gives them the assurance that Ogilvy can help Vodafone navigate not just the present, but also the needs of the future.

29

The Future of Advertising: Boom Time for Storytellers

As a young boy in Rajasthan, I was exposed to the phenomenal ancient art of storytelling: '*Pabuji ki phad*'. The phad was a painting, much like a storyboard used by advertising professionals or film-makers, on a long strip of cloth. A *bhopa* (bard) and *bhopi* (his wife) were the storytellers. Phad shows took place only after sunset, and this is how it went.

The phad was stretched and tied to two poles. The bhopa would begin narrating the epic story of Pabuji, the Rathod Rajput chief, using a stick in one hand to point to the particular 'frame' he was talking about. The bhopi would highlight the frame by the light of a lantern that she held in one hand.

The entertainers had to be extraordinarily quick-witted. If the bhopa sensed that the audience was losing interest in the narration, he would quickly skip a few frames to a more 'exciting' point in the story so that the audience stayed entertained. Imagine, content creators 'zapping' their own show. In essence, this is what phad artists did. Without having heard the phrase, they knew the meaning of 'audience engagement'.

This is the future of advertising: engaging audiences through great stories, albeit with the use of new technologies.

We live in a multimedia world of traditional and emerging media, ranging from print, radio, TV, cinema, outdoor, mobile, Internet, social media and content marketing; and we have no idea what the future might bring.

Consumers are changing with growing consumerism. They are becoming more aware of advertising and brands even as they are getting more socially conscious.

This new consumer is the new creative opportunity when seen in the context of the available media and technology.

No longer do we have to fight with the media planner for the additional five seconds that we need to tell a story well or tell it better. In the new media world, duration is history. YouTube, with its hundreds of millions of viewers, is a channel in its own right. We can now create communication of any length and make it available to the consumers. In addition, we have the DTH channels, where we can buy media at much lower prices than on traditional TV channels. We first used such DTH channels to air Tata Sky's four-minute 'jailbreak' commercial in 2013.

Today, all major advertisers look closely at these new channels and opportunities, with FMCG majors such as Unilever, Nescafé and Pepsi taking advantage of the cost-efficiency of YouTube and other digital media, even as financial brands like Birla Sun Life are jumping on the bandwagon.

All of you would have seen commercials like the Google Reunion search, Fortune Cooking Oil (*Do Chamach Dal*) and JSW Steel's 'Will of Steel' (featuring Geeta Phogat, winner of India's first-ever gold medal in women's wrestling, Commonwealth Games, 2010)—they all made a significant impact thanks to great storytelling that took advantage of the extra time that digital affords us.

Through the ages, great stories have needed patrons. In the old days, royalty like Akbar hired storytellers like Birbal, for example. Today, the list of 'patrons' has increased, as more and more categories, such as tourism and e-commerce back great, long stories.

Meanwhile, TV channels are going beyond cricket, promoting football and even ancient sports like kabaddi, creating more opportunities for storytelling.

The JSW Steel film reflects the passion and empowerment of the new small-town woman.

As this new media opportunity plays out, we witness society getting more educated and more conscious, breaking down taboos and old customs. In 1983, a commercial for Vicks Cough Drops that depicted my two-year-old niece was pulled off air, because in the TVC she winks at her father. Rules of the time forbade a woman to wink on TV!

In the new media world, duration is history.

Today's storytellers have no such problems as rules change, as society changes.

Media, especially social media, is giving rise to any number of debates on topics and subjects that were either ignored or brushed under the carpet. Today, women's rights, women's safety, gender equality, sexual harassment, gay rights, and corruption, to name a few, are part of daily public discourse. The fact that these subjects are being discussed in public forums allows brands and creatives to explore more emotional stories in a natural, non-contrived manner.

The JSW Steel film reflects the passion and empowerment of the new small-town woman, for example. Society is changing rapidly, and there are new triggers around us that we can spot and use to tell different types of stories while breaking stereotypes we have lived with for decades. As a society, we are now moving from empowering women to gender equality, and that's where the communication has to find inspiration as well.

These changes in society, and how advertising has reflected these changes, can be seen in the recent work we have done. The new Raga and Bournvita commercials show how advertising is portraying the new Indian woman and the changed mother–daughter relationship. Imagine, ten years ago a Bournvita ad without a young boy in it, in a setting other than a dining table or a kitchen, which is what we see in the new TVC, where the

Bournvita-drinking child is a daughter, not a son—and the mother is helping the daughter achieve her ambition to be a great boxer.

If women and girls are changing, so is the youth in the country. The youth today is getting socially conscious, with a point of view on all that happens in the country. The difference now is that the youth not only has an opinion, but also wants to express that opinion.

In the recent past, India, as a country, has been politically very charged. The political classes have come under scrutiny and have been the targets of vociferous criticism.

In 2013, we saw chaos in both houses of Parliament and in many state legislatures, and that provided the fodder for the commercial we did for *The Hindu*, warning politicians that the youth was watching them. It is due to the digital media that we were not constrained by the duration, and we could take all the time that was required to tell the story well.

Like everything else, parent–child relationships are changing as well. It is no longer the case that parents tell the children what to do and demand blind obedience. This is an era of new, mutual respect for each other, of greater transparency and closeness. All these changes are reflected in the communication that many brands are creating to be able to connect to the new consumer mindset.

In addition to these changes, marketers and brands are also seeking to build brand trust and brand reputation, trying to build 'goodwill' in addition to 'image'. Tata Tea used the successful 'Power of 49' to get women to vote during the last Lok Sabha elections (49 represented the percentage of women voters). While Tata Tea was the first to spot the opportunity, other brands jumped on the image bandwagon. Google created a campaign during the election provoking the first-time voter to exercise his or her franchise. Channel V ran a campaign asking the youth to wear seatbelts in cars. These are just a few examples of brands breaking away from traditional benefit-advertising to 'cause'-related advertising, a trend that marketers cannot ignore—because consumers relate positively to such communication.

Chaos in Parliament provided the fodder for the commercial we did for The Hindu.

If the content is interesting, entertaining and thought-provoking, consumers, in a way, become a distribution arm that amplifies the content by sharing it. We've all seen it with two videos that you would be familiar with—'Kolaveri Di' and 'Gangnam Style'. The first was designed to get consumers to share, while in the case of the second, the amplification was organic. As advertising professionals, it's the first that we have to focus on; we have no control over the second. That's the new challenge that agencies face. Now we can no longer be satisfied when we believe that an idea meets the brief; we have to ask ourselves another question. Is the idea share-worthy? Will the idea urge consumers to comment on it, to talk to the brand, to tweet about it?

If the content is interesting, entertaining and thought-provoking, consumers, in a way, become a distribution arm that amplifies the content by sharing it.

The convergence of media is a trigger for new creative thinking and ideas. A couple of years ago, Dove created what became an extraordinarily viral film by just getting a forensic expert to do sketches of women. The campaign, called 'Sketches', depicted women, first as seen by themselves and then as seen by another who had seen them for just a few minutes. Dove used this experiment to tell women 'You're more beautiful than you think'. The self-portraits were invariably 'uglier' than the 'other' portraits. Ten women were sketched; hundreds of thousands saw the sketches in exhibitions, and millions saw the experiment through viral videos and through media coverage. Media convergence is giving fresh oxygen to creatives to think of different ideas.

New media, new categories, evolving consumers, maturing marketers, convergence of media and technology are all stimulating new opportunities for advertising creativity and ideas.

We have never lived in more exciting times for creativity in advertising, and we continue to be in the storytelling business. However, we need to see ourselves as creators of content for channels that engage rather than as just creators of ads that are placed in the media.

Novelists or short-story writers, five-day players or T20 champions, everyone is welcome, and all content has an outlet. That's the new world we live in.

Just look at what technology has enabled in Broadway productions. I loved *The Lion King* and *War Horse* as movies. I was blown away by their Broadway presentations. But remember, behind both these great productions are great stories, great emotions and great meaning. Remove these and the productions are nothing but a mere display of technology. So, let us all look for stories from life and then take them to the consumer.

The future is bright. But let's all remember '*Pabuji ki phad*'. If the story is not great or if the story is not human, no technology will save you. Not today. Not any time in the future.

30

Beyond Advertising

Our greatest successes in recent years have come out of Ogilvy Activation. Activation created the most satisfying piece of work in recent years, the Lifebuoy Roti Reminder—and there are great lessons for both advertising and marketing professionals in the Roti Reminder.

When you embarked on a career in advertising or marketing, did you ever imagine that the greatest achievement of your life could be found in communicating on a roti at the Kumbh Mela? And that the communication would win awards—both for creativity and for effectiveness—at leading award platforms across the world, including at Cannes?

In the 1970s, a young creative would have thought of writing great lines for print or for radio, mostly in English. In the 1980s, it shifted to writing great scripts for TVCs as well—and in Hindi and other Indian languages as well. The demand grew beyond just great language; you needed to understand the cultural nuances as well of a broad variety of people. By the late twentieth century, we needed to reach people that conventional media could not reach.

That's what the 'Roti Reminder' was all about—reaching consumers efficiently without using conventional media.

Vipul Salvi was the young man who came up with the idea. Vipul, whom I had almost dismissed as 'just the guy who handles the creative for Activation, focusing on rural'.

And this is the man who came up with the greatest idea we've seen at Ogilvy India—greater than any idea I have ever come up with!

And, in a funny way, the roots of the ability to come up with an idea like this were planted more than three decades ago.

In the thirty-three years that I've been in the business of advertising, the responsibilities and remit of agencies have changed beyond recognition. In 1982, the job of agencies was to create communication for radio, TV, print, and outdoor, and plan and buy the relevant media. That was it.

That was the case even in 1982, though there were changes and developments afoot. Mani Aiyer kept an eye on the latest developments and practices globally so that all of us in India had a good idea of the impending changes. Thanks to David Ogilvy's interest and confidence in the efficiency of direct marketing, Mani was impressed enough to invest in the first direct marketing arm in an advertising agency in India. This was the beginning of Ogilvy's exploits and achievements in the one-on-one area. It's 2015 now, and almost all references to the phrase 'one-on-one' are made in the context of digital and Internet.

In Ogilvy, it's been different, thanks to Mani's vision and the support of clients such as Hindustan Lever (now Hindustan Unilever). Lever's needs in the early 1990s, paired with Ogilvy's global learnings saw the establishment of Ogilvy Outreach, which was set up to tackle the challenge of marketing in media-dark areas of India.

By the late 1990s, thanks to Ranjan Kapur's efforts we had a considerable presence in direct, PR and rural—and that saw us well positioned in one-on-one communication as more and more clients felt the need.

As communication evolved, so did our bouquet of offerings. Outreach was rechristened Ogilvy Activation. Our direct marketing wing became Ogilvy One. Once the digital revolution hit us, Ogilvy Digital and Ogilvy Social were born.

'Roti Reminder' is about reaching consumers efficiently without using conventional media.

In essence, while our core offering remained the creation of communication solutions using mass media to address client problems, we had developed expertise in the entire gamut of one-on-one communication, be it face-to-face, understanding e-commerce, communicating on social media and creating communication for the digital age, creating activation that could be amplified through digital and social, and so on.

Ten years from now, the industry will most certainly see new possibilities and opportunities—and new ways of communicating to consumers will have to evolve.

Everything evolves, and those who see it as a fluid scenario with different expressions, fresher and newer technology, are the people who are going to survive. Ideas will always prevail in this business, and that's what we need to remember. Whatever communication is created and for whatever medium it is created, at the core will be an idea.

The message is loud and clear: the kind of stuff that Ogilvy One and Ogilvy Digital did for Foxtime is made of legends—those were fantastic creative ideas. Ideas are not confined to television, ideas are not confined to print, ideas are not confined to anything—a big idea is a big idea, and a creative person must think of big ideas regardless of the medium that he is travelling on. Foxtime was a fantastic collaboration between what is known as Ogilvy advertising and Ogilvy digital.

Ideas will always prevail in this business, and that's what we need to remember. Whatever communication is created and for whatever medium it is created, at the core will be an idea.

But this chapter is not intended to be a plug for Ogilvy. I've used examples that I am familiar with to bring to life the fact that the communication challenges of today require many partners with many different competencies and skills to come together to come up with a viable solution.

Sometimes, these competencies might be available in a single company; sometimes the marketer might have to find them with different companies. The important thing to focus on is to ensure that all these different companies or divisions, which are all focused competency areas, do not become silos.

In Ogilvy, we ensure that the divisions strengthen each other; the 'advertising' division, for example, needs to think digital, and the 'digital' division needs to think advertising. In some years, the two will merge.

The silos are required—for a short period of time, till you gain expertise in a new area or technology or competency. Once that happens, the silo needs to get absorbed into the larger company and business.

'Silo' is not a bad word, as long as you ensure that the silo, after a period of time, ceases to be one. Having twenty silos simultaneously is a disaster, but having a new silo every year is almost a must, because it allows you to build new expertise in a rapidly changing environment.

Kunal Jeswani, now CEO of Ogilvy India, once headed our digital business. His job was to make all of us digitally sensitive, but not to make all of us savvy or experts. Younger people will be savvy, middle-aged people would be knowledgeable, older people like me should be supportive—Kunal's job was to make all of us digitally aligned and sensitive.

Will he convert me into a geek tomorrow morning? That would be an impossible job. What he can do is to convert me into a vociferous cheerleader of the digital capability.

Ogilvy One was once a silo. As times changed, it became a 'digital' Ogilvy One. Then we changed the name to reflect the changing times, and it was rechristened Ogilvy Digital. Much of the need for the change in name was to reflect the changing competencies, and much was to change clients' perception that Ogilvy One did only direct marketing in the old paradigm.

Today, this 'silo' is over 700 employees strong, addressing client needs in any area that requires one-on-one communication: mailers, emailers, activation, digital campaigns, social media, and so on.

All these 700 colleagues get one-on-one and digital, but they also understand brands and consumers. That's why Vipul was able to create the Roti Reminder.

That's the challenge in the business today; we need to create print ads and radio spots and TVCs—the legacy tools—and we also need to create the Roti Reminders. The trick is not to lose sight of either—the two need to coexist. The legacy businesses are still 88 per cent of the market, but the fastest growing business is digital.

It is the continuous creation of relevant silos, the sensitization of the entire agency to the new competencies that the silos focus on, and the absorption of these silos into the larger organization that decide the future of the company.

Creation of silos is like a cricketer going to the Dennis Lillee Fast Bowling Academy in Perth, Australia. Bowlers and batsmen go there, learning to either bowl brilliantly or handle great fast bowling. Once the techniques are learnt, the player returns, passing on the knowledge to his teammates. In a period of time, the whole team has a greater understanding of fast bowling, playing on fast pitches, and so on.

In a few years, a team competency develops—and there's no need to send bowlers to Perth any more.

For marketers who work with multiple communication partners, replace 'silos' with 'partners'. Each of the marketer's partners needs to understand the role of other partners. It's already happening. Now digital agencies understand more about brands and creativity, while creative agencies understand more about digital and social. Even out-of-home has had to reinvent itself with digital-out-of-home.

The more seamless the working relationship between silos or divisions or communication partners, the better the results for the marketer.

Afterword

Why I Never Started My Own Agency

NO, I AM NOT STARTING AN AGENCY OF MY OWN.

NO, I AM NOT JOINING ANOTHER AGENCY.

I HAVE NO INTENTION OR WISH TO WORK ANYWHERE OTHER THAN OGILVY.

Those who know me are aware of the fact that I do not raise my voice, but here I've taken the liberty of 'shouting' in print.

I could have made these statements many times in the past decade in response to rumours in the media, but they would have had little effect.

In India, media coverage on the advertising agency business focuses on speculation about who will resign from which agency or which agency will be sacked by which brand. In most instances, the 'news' is completely unfounded, even as the article carries authoritative quotes attributed to unnamed sources 'close to the developments'.

It is thus in the natural order of things that, as I turn sixty, the media speculate on my establishing my own advertising agency. Sections of the media have also linked me to the likely business to be launched by my nephew, Abhijit.

Before this book is published, there could be a few more articles making a few more completely baseless speculations on my life after Ogilvy.

Interestingly, many senior journalists who have encouraged the gossip columns on my impending move have since moved on to other options, even as I remain in Ogilvy.

Speculation on my leaving Ogilvy is recent as far as the media is concerned, but over the past twenty years I've been asked numerous times why I don't start my own agency.

The answer has remained the same.

Some years ago, a much respected industrialist pulled me aside at a party we were attending and told me, 'I have never met a bigger idiot than you in my life. Why don't you start a business of your own instead of working for Martin Sorrell? We need an Indian agency that goes international, and who is better placed than you to start one? I'll fund you and I'll give you all the office space that you need.'

As far as I am concerned, money and office space are not essential elements to start an advertising agency—belief and philosophy are.

My background has defined me in so many ways. One of them is that I am not a loner—I am a team player, both literally and otherwise. From the time I was in school, I chose team sports, preferring cricket and football to golf and tennis.

I joined Ogilvy and felt the same comfort as I felt at home. Everyone was family. Everyone contributed to our success; everyone was together in difficult times. Over the decades, I have worked with many colleagues who are family to me, even if some have left the agency and moved on elsewhere. I've never felt the need to even think of moving on. Ogilvy has been home to me, and will always be.

In the late nineties, a senior executive from one of WPP's largest competitors and I met, by appointment, at the Taj Lands End in Bombay. In a short meeting, he proposed that they would like to invest in an agency that I start. I asked him why I should start an agency, and his answer was, 'We'll put your name on the board.'

In response, I told him that, on his way from the airport to the hotel, he would have passed at least twenty billboards with Ogilvy's work on them. While he didn't see my name on any of those billboards, my work is shouting from each and every one of them.

The short meeting caused me to think of the reasons that would cause anyone to leave a company and start one on their own.

The first would be if the current company did not allow you to actualize your potential. The second would be if the company underpaid you. The third would be the 'name on the board' thing.

If I ask myself these questions, my answers are quick in coming. In all these years at Ogilvy, I have never felt like an employee. In my younger days, I felt like a younger member of the family. In my leadership days, I felt like the owner of the company.

I joined Ogilvy and felt the same comfort as I felt at home. Everyone was family. Everyone contributed to our success; everyone was together in difficult times.

Was I allowed to actualize my potential? Throughout my career, I have had the unstinting support of my seniors and colleagues. Many of my seniors have advised me, mentored me and encouraged me in my experiments, and supported my decisions. It is *because* of Ogilvy that I have been able to achieve all that I have.

For many people in the world, no amount of money is enough.

As far as I am concerned, I do not have endless needs and wants, so it is easier for me to be 'satisfied' on the money issue. As a young boy I had never dreamt that I would reach where I have reached or earn as much as I earn today. With these reference points, I have been looked after beyond my expectations. Money has not been the deciding factor in any decision that I have taken. I used to wonder what people do with the millions more than they need—they will need to live for much longer than the average lifespan to spend those extra millions. I am satisfied with how I have been rewarded financially, so reason number two to leave Ogilvy and start my own company doesn't work either.

We come to reason number three: having your name on the board.

How important is it to have your name on the board? I am very proud of the fact that the name Ogilvy is on my board. I am very proud of the fact that lots of people in India and around the world have complimented me on some of the good work that I have done. My name is my work. In any case, normally roads are named after people posthumously. If you are dead, you don't really care.

I have been allowed to feel like the owner of a company. Once I feel like an owner, the 'name on the board' carrot ceases to be a carrot. When it's my company, everyone knows it is mine.

So none of the three big reasons to leave has applied to me all these years; none applies to me today. I've reached a stage where I have Ogilvy in my blood, and that will never go away.

I'm sixty, I'm fit, I'm healthy and driven. If I do decide to do something other than Ogilvy, it'll be a retirement passion or a hobby. It could be to help India be a better place. It could be mentoring youngsters in communication or it could be a full-time job—spreading rumours about which journalist is going to join which publication.

Acknowledgements

I would like to thank:

- All clients past and present who trusted me and my team with their brands.
- All my colleagues at Ogilvy, past, and present, juniors and seniors, for the body of work we created together.
- All film-makers and their extended teams of artists right up to the spot boys who made our ideas come alive.
- Music directors, singers, voice-over artists.
- Photographers and printers.
- Media and industry bodies in India and the world who celebrated our efforts and encouraged us to keep improving.
- My friends and family who I borrowed life from.
- People of India for inspiring me.
- My parents for being there for me.
- My friend Sunil Doshi for relentlessly persuading me to write this book and for liaising with the publisher on all the necessary paperwork.
- My partner, Rajiv Rao, for the cover design and inputs on overall design.
- The distinguished photographer Suresh Natarajan for the cover image.

- My teachers at NVD Balmandir, St. Xavier's School, Jaipur, and St. Stephen's College, Delhi, and all my cricket coaches.
- My colleagues and seniors who taught me my cricket.
- Penguin Random House for making this book happen.